PAMELA STEELE
FOREWORD BY BENEBELL WEN

ETERNAL *Seeker* ORACLE

INSPIRED BY THE TAROT'S MAJOR ARCANA

REDFeather™
MIND | BODY | SPIRIT

4880 Lower Valley Road, Atglen, PA 19310

Other Schiffer Books on Related Subjects:

White Witch Tarot, Maja D'Aoust, ISBN 978-0-7643-5367-3
Tarot of the Moors, Gina G. Thies, ISBN 978-0-7643-5609-4

Copyright © 2021 by Pamela Steele

Library of Congress Control Number: 2020943399

All rights reserved. No part of this work may be reproduced or used in any form or by any means—graphic, electronic, or mechanical, including photocopying or information storage and retrieval systems—without written permission from the publisher.

The scanning, uploading, and distribution of this book or any part thereof via the Internet or any other means without the permission of the publisher is illegal and punishable by law. Please purchase only authorized editions and do not participate in or encourage the electronic piracy of copyrighted materials.

"Red Feather Mind Body Spirit" logo is
a trademark of Schiffer Publishing, Ltd.
"Red Feather Mind Body Spirit Feather" logo is
a registered trademark of Schiffer Publishing, Ltd.

Type set in Tomarik/Affair/Minion Pro*

ISBN: 978-0-7643-6125-8
Printed in China

Published by Red Feather Mind, Body, Spirit
An imprint of Schiffer Publishing, Ltd.
4880 Lower Valley Road
Atglen, PA 19310
Phone: (610) 593-1777; Fax: (610) 593-2002
E-mail: Info@schifferbooks.com
Web: www.redfeathermbs.com

For our complete selection of fine books on this and related subjects, please visit our website at www.schifferbooks.com. You may also write for a free catalog.

Schiffer Publishing's titles are available at special discounts for bulk purchases for sales promotions or premiums. Special editions, including personalized covers, corporate imprints, and excerpts, can be created in large quantities for special needs. For more information, contact the publisher.

We are always looking for people to write books on new and related subjects. If you have an idea for a book, please contact us at proposals@schifferbooks.com.

To Family, Friends, and Seekers
who have traveled this Path with me;
May this Oracle become the Rosetta Stone
to understanding the Language of your Soul.
May you become what you choose
to experience.

Believe in your infinite potential.
Your only limitations are
those you set upon yourself.

—ROY T. BENNETT

Contents

Foreword by Benebell Wen 5
Eternal Seeker Oracle Readers' Ethics 7
What Is an Oracle? 8
The Care and Feeding of Your Oracle Deck 10
Keeping a Journal 11
Composing Questions 12
Shuffling and Dealing the Cards 13
Oracle Card Spreads 14
The Cards
    1~The Seeker 22
    2~Magus 25
    3~The Oracle 28
    4~Divine Feminine 31
    5~The Crone 34
    6~Elder Gods 37
    7~Tradition 40
    8~Choices 43
    9~Sacred Alignment 46
    10~Soul Fire 49
    11~Spirit Guide 52
    12~Wheel of Time 55
    13~The Law 58
    14~Perception 61
    15~The Traveler 64
    16~Harmony 67
    17~Attachments 70

    18~Chaos 73
    19~Hope 76
    20~Inspiration 79
    21~Intuition 82
    22~Heart Song 85
    23~Rebirth 88
    24~Attainment 91
    25~The Weaver 94
    26~The Universe 97
    27~Truth 100
    28~Shadows 103
    29~The Guardian 106
    30~Wisdom 109
    31~Emergence 112
    32~Infinity 115
    33~I AM 118
    Fibonacci Spiral 120

From the Oracle's Creator 121
Acknowledgments 123
Resources 124
References 127
Quotes 128

Foreword

Pamela Steele is a true sorceress of portals. Her art takes you to another world, one of dragons, mages, and enchantment. *Eternal Seeker Oracle* reads as if a wise woman sits tenderly by my side, whispering foresight. The deck conveys a strong, honored sense of tradition, veneration of our elders in the Craft, and what it means to be the eternal seeker.

Steele's first deck, published back in 2007, *Steele Wizard Tarot*, featured a fantasy art style reminiscent of the role-playing games that bring me nostalgia, not to mention that her works seem to be particularly well suited for pathworking. I have remained a loyal fan of Pamela's work ever since. The *Eternal Seeker Oracle* marks an evolution of the artist's work, transitioning into the digital medium but still featuring the dreamlike elements that Steele's art is so well known for.

I've been keeping the thirty-three-card deck on my office desk, weighted in place by a piece of natural iolite. Every morning when I sit down with my first mug of coffee, I'll pull a card for myself from *Eternal Seeker*. The deck truly yields the most-magnificent readings. The keyword on the card I pull becomes the essence of magic that gets woven through the events of my day.

Compact enough to tuck into a tote and take with you on your physical journeys through life, this is a deck for imparting everyday guidance. Steele's thaumaturgic art dances to life as you read the cards for a friend over tea. The cards bring a moment of miracle between strangers when that passerby stops, sits down at your table at the fair, and gets a fifteen-minute reading from you. Both the casual and the professional reader will find their roots and their totemic heart in *Eternal Seeker*.

Eternal Seeker invites us to revisit the Old World Tarot tradition of divining with the Majors only, though Steele has included eleven additional Spirit-inspired cards to the traditional twenty-two. The numerology of thirty-three cards signifies the revelation of that which was concealed. Occultists associate the number 33 with sacred teachings, the Holy Trinity, and the Triple Goddess. The number 33 is the mirror of a trinity on Earth reflecting the trinity of Heaven.

I am entranced by the mysteries of this deck. In the current marketplace, saturated with passing trends and oracle decks bustling with the zeal of the modern maiden, *Eternal Seeker* will be your sage grandmother embracing you with timeless, timeworn words of wisdom. My admiration for what *Eternal Seeker* accomplishes and will accomplish for time immemorial knows no bounds.

Three years ago, I met Pamela Steele at a Tarot conference and I got along with her immediately. She is a straight-shooting, sprightly, and outspoken firebrand with a kind heart, loving nature, and a peculiar rubric of honesty that's going extinct in our world. Yet, I am grateful for her decks, especially *Eternal Seeker*, because it will memorialize for all of perpetuity this rare and beautiful gusto that is the signature of Pamela Steele. This deck is an invitation to you to engage with your ancestors. It will be a treasured oracle that connects an old-school generation of diviners with the new.

Pamela Steele is one of the most talented card readers I know, and she passes those gifts on to you through this incredible Tarot-inspired oracle deck. When you hold this deck in your hands, you inherit the psychic agility of real-life wizardry. She is the elder who will mentor the new generation of seekers on pagan spirituality and divination. *Eternal Seeker Oracle* is a marvel to behold. Its otherworldly quality will conjure in you a clairsentience you did not even realize you possessed.

—BENEBELL WEN

Author: *Holistic Tarot, The Tao of Craft*;
artist/author: *The Spirit Keeper's Tarot, The Book of Maps*

READERS' ETHICS

You always have the right to exercise your own Free Will and to make your own Choices.

You are entitled to full and complete answers to the questions covered in your reading.

Your reading is private and confidential.

Oracle readers do not make your decisions for you.

It is recommended that you seek competent legal, medical, or financial advice from a qualified professional if your questions are of those natures.

What Is an Oracle?

A dictionary describes an Oracle thus:

"Especially in ancient Greece an utterance, often ambiguous or obscure, given by a priest or priestess at a shrine as the response of a god to an inquiry."

"The agency or medium giving such responses."

"A shrine or place at which such responses were given: *the oracle of Apollo at Delphi.*"

That being noted, for our purposes, this Oracle is a thirty-three-card deck of playing cards inspired by the *Steele Wizard Tarot*'s Major Arcana. The *Steele Wizard Tarot*, in turn, was inspired by the 1910 edition of the *Rider-Waite-Smith Tarot*. Therefore, this Oracle is the product of an evolutionary process whereby the designer/creator (yours truly, Pamela Steele) has chronicled her personal Journey of four decades through the Tarot's Major Arcana. In order to "fill in the gaps," eleven additional cards have been added to Tarot's traditional twenty-two-card Majors. Six of the cards are from the *Steele Wizard Tarot*, plus an additional five cards. To simplify, if you're familiar with the *Rider-Waite-Smith* (or the *Steele Wizard*) *Tarot*'s Major Arcana, employing this Oracle should be effortless. An Oracle may also be used in conjunction with any other Tarot deck to augment and amplify readings.

An Oracle may be used to divine the future, gain insights into situations or persons, and seek advice both for personal and spiritual dilemmas. Although it's not exactly designed for fortune-telling, there are some who do use Oracles for that purpose. When your intent is pure and your focus is clear, there is no incorrect way to approach the Oracle.

This Oracle was specifically designed to assist the Eternal Seeker (you or your client) in studying, knowing, and understanding life. The images, although inspired by the Major Arcana, seek to delve into the core authenticity of the archetypes that is reflected by the title of each card. Each part of the images represents something unique and specific. From the colors to the smallest details, the symbols speak on a soul-deep level to help you intuit and identify the underlying and often-motivational meanings of your life. This provides you with a platform from which to launch the next stage of your Personal Journey. The *Eternal Seeker Oracle* was created as a personal tool to enable you to once and for all lay to rest old hurts, confusion, and emotional ties that no longer serve who you are now. It was created to assist you in gathering the parts of yourself and your soul that have been devastated, wounded, and forgotten. Only by collecting all the missing pieces and healing them can you finally, fully become whole.

When you first begin consulting an Oracle, you may rely on what is written in this book for "guidelines" to understand the meanings of the cards. They are named "guidelines" because as you become more familiar with your Oracle, you may find that the symbols have specific meanings to you that may or may not be found in any book. As you study the Oracle, you will find the pictures speak to your soul, and they will speak on a very authentic level in a unique way that you may or may not hear with your ears. You will know it deep within your heart where beyond any doubt what you *feel* about that card is very real and completely authentic. As your skills with an Oracle grow, the images on the cards will begin to blend together in your heart, your mind, and your soul. Then, rather than read each one, in turn, you will intuitively know the story behind the pictures and the wisdom they have to impart. From the first to the last, the soul-deep knowledge gathered will be yours to enact as you will.

The Care and Feeding of Your Oracle Deck

You are now the auspicious owner of your very own *Eternal Seeker Oracle*! It is important, as with all divination tools, to keep your cards safe and protected. When you are not using them, they may be wrapped in silk or kept in a cloth bag large enough to hold them comfortably. You may also choose to store them in a box between readings. The box should be large enough to hold your cards and their silk wrapping or bag. Some readers prefer silk bags for their cards, since it is widely known to help protect the cards from unwanted influences, depending on your reading area. Truthfully, most natural fabrics are appropriate for storing and carrying your cards. Besides, if you find the perfect bag or box, and it's absolutely too good to pass up no matter what it's made from, there's nothing to stop you from purifying the energies, blessing the lovely bag or box, and keeping your Oracle cards safely tucked inside.

Some readers never allow the Seeker (the person asking the question) to handle or even touch their cards. I am not one of those readers. It's usually not a good idea to let someone else shuffle your cards, since Oracle decks tend to be much larger than other decks. Mishandling during shuffling can and will result in damage to the cards. Damage can be kept at a minimum by using the shuffling method described in this book. However, to get started I generally ask the client to clear their thoughts and hold the cards prior to shuffling, or I simply ask them to blow on them. Yes, silly as it sounds, gently blowing on them works really well. After I shuffle the cards, I offer them to the client to cut into three piles and restack the deck. By that point, I'm clear on what spread we will be using and how many cards we'll need to start. Then rather than begin dealing the cards, I fan the cards face down on the table and ask the client to choose the number of cards we will need for the spread we'll be using. Watch closely as they pass their hand over the cards. As each card is chosen and added to the assigned pile to be used, the client is doing their own job of choosing, shuffling, and organizing the data. After I have finished reading, before putting my cards away, I gently blow on them myself to make sure there are no unwanted energies attached from the reading they just gave.

The more you work and play with your cards, the more in tune you will become with one another. Also, the better you get to know and understand each other, the better connected you will be and the more proficient you will become at your readings.

Shall we continue?

Keeping a Journal

Keeping a record of your Oracle journey is vital although not mandatory. You may believe that your memory is infallible and you will remember, but you're going to be covering more information than you think possible. At times it may even feel like you're doing everything you can to stay ahead of an avalanche. So don't trust just your memory. Write it down. It will help you learn about yourself in ways you cannot imagine. You can use a notebook or a binder, or you can find a custom blank-page book in which to write your notes. You may even have a program on your laptop or tablet where you can create your journal.

    Why is it important? For example, let's say you drew a card from your deck and didn't understand what it was trying to tell you. Go ahead and write the date, time, and any and all information about the card in your journal. If you used a spread, write down which card fell in which position, and make notes of the positions too. You can copy from the book, but also remember to write how it makes you *feel*. After all, we're looking for authenticity, and learning how to identify and name the feelings you're experiencing will be priceless as you move forward and grow. In just a few weeks, or days, or hours, something will click and you will think "a-HA! That's what the card meant!" Then you can go back and add more to your journal for that card. Just for the sake of clarity, don't expect the clouds to part and bathe you in a shower of golden light while little cherubs slowly descend playing heavenly music on harps and trumpets. But do expect the inner light to suddenly flip on. With practice and patience, this on/off switch will eventually evolve into what you may think of as more like a dimmer switch. Instead of being either go or no-go, the inner light will always be on, glowing faintly in the background and waiting for you to turn it up or down as needed. Eventually, the secret whispers of the Oracle will be a comfortable companion instead of a strange foreigner who drinks all of your tea and props their feet on your coffee table.

    Take your time. Be patient. You will succeed.

Composing Questions

Over the past four-plus decades of divination reading, I have noticed that most people have questions. I have also noticed that for whatever reason, they generally do not ask right away. Most times they are a bit shy about asking, and that's okay. When I begin reading, I assure them that if at any time during the reading something is unclear, please speak up and ask. This opens the way for them to have any part of the reading clarified.

The Oracle should be approached with clear thoughts and the intent of seeking advice from the inner realms. How the question is phrased is very important. The clearer the question is defined, the clearer the answer will be. For example: If the Seeker wants to know if they should study medicine or art, the question should be "Would it be best for me to study _____?" Not "Should I study medicine or art?" What you're doing by refining and directing your focused question is taking what would constitute a scattergun and turning it into a laser beam.

If you want the more informed answer, phrase your question carefully. It is also important to note that if someone wants a reading and that person is really upset, your cards are not going to be clear in the answer they give you. They will pick up the chaotic energies of mixed and upset emotions, and you will get a mixed and upset reading with little to no decisive answers. At times like this, it's best to wait awhile until everyone is emotionally calmer and a bit clearer.

Also, always go with the first cards that appear. It will do you no good to keep asking the same question different ways, hoping for a different answer. All it will do is annoy the cards, and they will start giving you "attitude." Honestly. Oh, and another thing: readings are about the person you are reading for and no one else. They are not for eavesdropping or spying on someone, nor for snooping on your children or your spouse. We're consulting an Oracle, not a private investigator.

Shuffling and Dealing the Cards

The first thing to do is relax and clear your mind. Take a few deep breaths and just let everything around you dissolve. Focus and clarity are the only ingredients needed for an authentic accurate Oracle consultation. Now let's get started!

Some readers prefer that the cards remain in their upright positions for a reading. This means the pictures on the cards are never upside down or "reversed." Other readers feel that limits the reading. These are your cards. Use your instincts on this issue. I believe that using reversals adds more depth and clarity to readings, so I use them. Besides, reversals don't necessarily dictate that the card means the opposite of the upright meaning. It is a variation or modification of the meaning, and some cards are less intense in their reversed position.

In order to blend the cards both with upright and reversed pictures, the method that works best for me begins by turning my left hand with my fingers pointing toward me to cut the deck. After picking up about half the cards, I then turn my fingers, holding the cut cards away from me. This reverses the cards I just cut from the deck with one motion. Next, I pick up the rest of the cards with my right hand, fingers resting lightly on the table, thumbs toward the center. Then I position the two halves close enough together to allow them to gently fall together, side by side, rather than forcibly bending and riffling them. It is easier on your cards not to bend them when shuffling. This takes practice, but handling your cards will give you the feel for them, and you will master this technique quickly. If you have another way that suits you better, by all means, use that one. Everyone has his or her own way of "shuffling the question into the deck." (Note: I always keep the cards facedown when shuffling.)

Remember to treat them gently, and you will both be a lot happier.

The cards are then cut into three piles (again using your left hand). If you choose not to let the Seeker handle the cards, you may now have them point to which pile they choose to be read. Some people will hold their left hands just above the three piles (without touching them) to see if they can feel any warmth or vibration coming from a specific pile. The cards are then restacked, with the chosen cards on top, into a single pile.

Place the stacked deck to your left side on the table for easy access, but far enough away that it's not in the way of where your cards will be laid out for the reading. Using your left hand, take the top card off your deck, turning it over side to side to reveal the face of the card. Turning the cards over side to side keeps the upright or reverse position of the card as it is removed from the deck. This is important. If you flip the card top to bottom or bottom to top to show the picture, it will reverse the card image. If you are using multiple cards in a spread, continue taking cards in this manner from the top of the deck.

Once all your cards are on the table, the remaining cards in the deck can stay in a stack off to the side. Keep them within an easy reach just in case you need to lay an extra card for any reason. Now we begin!

Oracle Card Spreads

"To spread or not to spread?" That is the question. Some readers prefer a more structured approach to their readings, while others let the cards fall where they may and follow their own path, dancing to their own drummer. Either way is absolutely 100% correct. What is important is the clarity with which you approach your Oracle.

In simpler words, the clearer your thoughts and focus, the clearer the reading will be. Some readers have or will devise a ritual to perform before they approach the Oracle. This is also up to you, and no one can dictate terms when it comes to your preferred approach, with human or animal sacrifice being noted exceptions, of course. The important points to remember are "focus and clarity."

Getting to know your Oracle does involve a bit more than shaking hands or meeting for coffee a couple of times. When you're ready to read, one of the most direct ways to begin to interact with your Oracle is a straightforward attitude. These are situations where you will pull one card per question or statement. Here are a few suggestions as to basic thoughts that might get you started. Simply and honestly ask or state the following:

1. "What advice do you have for me today?"

2. "I seek your guidance."

3. "What most needs my attention?"

Of course, you can pull a second card for more information or clarification for the first card, but that can, and generally does, lead to even more confusion. Instead, perhaps try a simple three-card spread to connect to your Inner Divinity and find the clues or answers you're seeking. Remember, it is all about clarity and focus. Therefore, "huh?" does not qualify as a valid question.

Three-Card Spreads
Then-Now-Tomorrow Spread

1. Explore the events, circumstances, and contributors of your past. Fully appreciate every millisecond of every heartbeat that it took to bring you to this here and now. Without those exact, specific experiences, you would not be who you are now. Who you are now is perfect.

2. Here is a reflection of the person you have become. This is who you were meant to be at this place in time. No other is qualified to be here at this exact moment. You and your contributions are vital to the whole. Embrace your authenticity.

3. As you travel your path you will evolve and become "more" than your wildest dreams. If this card represents where you believe and know your path to lie, please continue and change nothing. If this is not your path, seek alternate routes.

Tomorrow
Who you are in the process of becoming if nothing changes.

Now
The most authentic you at this time.

Then
What happened in the past that motivated you to be here and now.

Oracle Card Spreads

Strength-Challenge-Direction Spread

1. Here you find where your greatest strength lies. You will seek to find its limits, its depths, and, above all else, the source of that strength. When we are tested, we may often feel we have reached the limit of what strength we have. By knowing the source of that strength, you will find its access beyond limitless.

2. The challenge for each of us is to apply our strengths where they are the most effective. Even anger can be considered a strength if it is controlled and used as a tool, as opposed to you being the tool . . . just sayin'.

3. Properly applied strength can and will present opportunities that were previously denied. Now that you can utilize your own inner strength properly, doors will open and your path becomes clear. This is the direction that will allow you to seize the moment.

Direction
Where your path leads from meeting your recent challenge.

Challenge
Where your strength should be applied for maximum effect.

Strength
Where your greatest strength is sourced.

Reaching Your Potential

1. Here is where you are right now. This is all about you and your journey and has little to nothing to do with anyone else. Don't try to read any other influence into this scenario, be it a person, animal, mineral, or vegetable.

2. This is a "to-do" card. Here are the details of what you need to actually, physically do to get to where you're going. Even if it's as mundane as getting a bus pass, checking your ticket, or fueling up your vehicle, get busy!

3. The carousel is coming around again, and this time it's your turn to grab that brass ring. Do so with both hands and own it. This is who you are now. Not who you were or not who others say you are . . . this is the truth of who you are becoming.

Your Potential
What must be realized and embraced to fulfill your destiny.

Your Path
Where you are in your personal journey.

Action Needed
What must change or alter to continue forward.

Four-Card Spread
What Needs My Attention?

1. What is right in front of you that you may or may not be seeing? Take a close look at your situation and your surroundings. You're tripping over something repeatedly that needs to be addressed.

2. Here is the Big Picture. Take a step back and see what surrounds you objectively and without judgment. In other words, see the forest, not the trees.

3. This is what will take you by the hand and walk you through the situation. Think of it as your new best friend and companion who sincerely does have your best interests at heart.

4. If you honestly want to put this to rest, here's what you need. Let it sink in and it will make sense, if it doesn't already. Clear your thoughts and take care of business.

What Needs My Attention?

Advice

Overview   Guidance

What needs my attention?

Five-Card Spreads
"Shining the Light and Moving Forward" Spread

1. The easiest person to lie to is you. This card will shine a light on what you're ignoring or refusing to see. Self-honesty is mandatory in Self-Mastery.

2. What brought you here? Something in your history has directed you to this exact moment in time, and here is where you need to be. What was that event? Who was that masked person?

3. Remember, no matter where you go, here you are. This card looks closely at your current situation. Look carefully. This is your new starting point.

4. How to move forward isn't always clear. This card shows the most beneficial way to focus your thoughts and set your intentions. Listen to your Inner Divinity.

5. Every leg of your journey begins with a single step. Consider what it took to bring you here, and take the next step with confidence.

Oracle Card Spreads

"Dreams vs. Reality" Spread

1. Well, here you are. Take a good, long look at your current situation. Then take an inventory of what you have to work with from this point forward.

2. What are you not saying? What defines your deepest, darkest secrets? What are you keeping hidden even from you?

3. Castles in the air or the creative muse's inspiration? What constitutes your dreams? Where do your thoughts go when left unattended?

4. We cannot all be princesses. Someone has to stand on the sidelines and cheer when the carriage passes by. Or perhaps we (the Royal We) can be the princess.

5. If you're going to stay sane and keep fueling your dreams, this is what needs to happen. This is who you need to become. If this is part of your Master Plan, then go for it. If not, you might want to jump ship and try a different plan.

One of the reasons I like using spreads is because it's a predetermined map. The positions tell me what I'm looking for, and the card fills in the details. You can and, I hope, will create your own spreads to use with this oracle. You may also use it in traditional Tarot spreads. Or you may choose to use it for deeper insights in conjunction with your favorite Tarot (or Lenormand) deck while reading. But come what may, let your personal Muse and your Goddess-given (or God-given) intuition guide you through the process. Remember, there is no wrong way to read, and this companion book is only a guideline.

The main goal is to have fun with all of it. Find joy. Live in your happy place. Let the Oracle speak as a companion and a guide. Treat your Oracle as a friend and companion. Remember, though, that the Oracle is paper and ink and not written on stone. It's okay to argue with friends.

To sum it all up, the words that were written for the *Steele Wizard Tarot* apply here as well:

Hold the Keys to Self-Knowledge.

Unlock the Mysteries of your Personal Reality.

Begin the Journey to Self-Discovery, Self-Empowerment, and Self-Mastery.

And may you always enjoy your Journey.

Pamela Steele

1 The Seeker

Wherever you are on your Journey is always the beginning.

Inspired by Tarot's "Fool." Numbered 1, the starting point is always with one's self.

The Seeker is the personification of our spiritual quest for wholeness. For this sacred journey, we need to be aware of our birth gifts. When we are born, each of us arrives with what may be thought of as a Spiritual Toolbox. As we make our way in life, we delve into the toolbox and discover what is inside. For instance, upon opening, you may find a hammer and a paintbrush. Your thoughts go immediately to "A hammer! A paintbrush! I shall become a carpenter!" But looking deeper inside the box, and observing your surroundings in your growing life, you may find that the paintbrush comes with a pallet, an easel, and oil paints. The hammer is next to hardware for hanging paintings, which brings the epiphany that you are not a carpenter as you first believed. Perhaps you are an artist who will change the way the world sees itself.

Every Journey begins with a single step, sometimes chosen with or without planning, thought, or even preparation. Often lacking clear direction, the Journey becomes a Quest for knowledge, experience, and eventually wisdom. It is a Spiritual Need that drives the Seeker to step onto a path and follow that road where it leads. The way may be fraught with danger, and sacrifices may be required. But a youthful soul and a joyful heart welcome the challenges set forth by the unknown. For it is only through experience with the unfamiliar that we learn and grow. Also worth mentioning is we often learn more from what we perceive as failures than we do from our assumed successes. Knowing when to begin, or continue, one's Sacred Journey can be indicated by any number of clues. For example, when one's parents wrap one's lunch in a road map, with a compass attached to the ring where one's house key used to hang, is generally a signal for the Seeker to get on the road. Henceforth, after lunch, the map may be used as a guideline rather than a set course.

From deep in an ancient forest, a walking staff fashioned from a fallen oak is magically adorned with a living white rose, signifying the blossoming of Spirit, and serves to steady one's feet on the often-uneven path. To aid us along the way, we collect companions, antagonists, and protagonists. To accommodate our Seeker, a newly hatched alabaster dragon rests comfortably on the young wizard's shoulder, signifying the birth of true wisdom, with the added bonus of eventually being able to scorch any vicious attackers or people who generally annoy the traveler. Trotting along beside the Seeker is a white wolf pup exploring its surroundings but always remaining nearby, bringing loyalty, companionship, and familial ties. The mischievous snow-colored bobcat kitten's curiosity, playfulness, and honed natural instincts alert the Seeker to be aware of their surroundings, with a reminder to make time to play. A Lemurian crystal lights the fork in the road where the Seeker must now choose a direction. All options are open.

Guidelines: A journey into the unknown. Here we find the beginning of wisdom as we gather knowledge. Driven by a great desire to accomplish wonderful goals, the Spirit seeks growth and development through experience. The journey brings occasion for new opportunities and unlimited possibilities. Take stock of your surroundings and what assets you currently have at your disposal. Choose your next step with care and allow your destiny to manifest.

Reversed: Innocence, thoughtless action, indiscretion, and inexperience are indicated. Fear of the unknown may hold the Seeker back from a wonderful new experience. Not listening to your instincts creates poor choices or a wrong turn. The choices have been based on fear as opposed to a feeling of safety. Stubbornness is not the same as determined perseverance. Nor will beating your head against a brick wall create the desired doorway.

Notes:

2 Magus

As you think, you create.

Inspired by the Tarot's "Magician," the number 2 stands with one foot in each world.

As we think, we create. Everything, everyone, begins with a thought. With a thought, we explore our power of creation. With a thought, we comprehend that what surrounds us is, to a certain extent, of our own making. How else but by claiming ownership can we each change our small corner of the world? By examining and understanding our inner dialogue (you know, the constant chatter that's the background noise of our lives), we begin to pay attention to how we're programming our creative processes. We begin by not letting the "white noise" in your head lull you into complacency, but by changing thought patterns one by one. Thoughts create energy. Energy creates mass. Mass creates form.

The Magus has learned to focus his thoughts and direct his will toward creation. Within each of us lies the inborn ability to create. All we need is clarity of thought and focus of intent. Our planet, our cultures, our religions, and all that exist are cocreations of Divine Beings (us) having human experiences in conjunction with the Creator of All That Is. When the pure light of Divinity enters the material, it fractures into an infinite number of colors we call emotions. Using our personalized palettes, we color our world, giving it depth and meaning. Always, the most-authentic emotions are the brightest and most powerful. The Magus has mastered the ability to access this formidable energy and bend it to his will.

The Magus may be the tribe's Shaman, Wise Woman, Healer, or any title pertaining to the ability to enter the worlds beyond our physical reality and bring valuable, life-giving knowledge to the people. To illustrate, a young child was observing his aunt as she coaxed an injured hawk into allowing her to approach it and free it from a wire fence. After calming the wild bird, she was then able to assess its wing and smooth the bent feathers. Once she was sure there was no real damage, just a few displaced feathers and much righteous indignation from the young hawk, she moved it away from danger and stepped back. The feral bird took a couple of steps, looked back at the woman, nodded its head, and took flight. The child's mother remarked, "Your Auntie is certainly good at doing magic." The boy looked at his mother and replied, "Auntie doesn't do magic, Mom. She is magic."

With the Staff of Power bearing a glowing crystal, the Magus is able to direct the powers of Creation to bring authentic emotions into being and to manifest what is desired. The Rune Sword hangs from his belt, with inscriptions defining the clarity of thought that separates what is necessary from what is superfluous. The chalice at his feet overflows with the undiluted essence of Spirit as it forms the material world. The Magus wears a snow-white robe to denote the purity of thought, action, and intent. Around his shoulders flows a crimson cape representing his passion. A golden pentagram hangs on his chest, keeping his heart connected to the world he serves. Remember to pay particular attention to our thoughts. What we think determines what we feel. What we feel constructs our beliefs. Our beliefs determine the colors with which we paint our world.

Guidelines: The ability to create what is desired. Talent and resources are at your command, and all you need do is grasp the opportunity with both hands. Define your intent, focus your will, and unleash your full potential. Power, talent, skill, and the ability to concentrate are all indicated.

Reversed: The misuse of power causes projects to crumble and fail. You have been or are being deceived by one whose intent is to manipulate. A project fails due to unauthentic emotions fueling the intention. Lack of clarity and harmful emotions sabotage the efforts for positive changes. Redefine your purpose and intent.

Notes:

3 The Oracle

Know thyself.

Inspired by the Tarot's "High Priestess." The number 3 represents the Triple Goddess.

Delving into the oceans of collective consciousness doesn't necessarily require scuba gear, but it does help to be prepared. As with all Oracles, many of the messages received will be vague, ambiguous, or even obscure to most rational minds. Consider the words inscribed over the temple of the famed Oracle of Delphi. The first inscription reads, "Know Thyself" and was later clarified by the philosopher Socrates, who professed that "The unexamined life is not worth living." Another less known of the Delphic maxims is "Nothing to excess." It truly is all about knowing your limits and using that knowledge as a measure of self-control. Insights, intuition, instincts, and deep knowing are all attributes that when honed to perfection allow you to easily access your own innate knowledge buried deep within your psyche.

    The Oracle is the personification of mystery, the unknown, and even the unknowable. She is the archetypical mediator between humanity and our Creator. However, to request guidance from the Oracle is essentially to consult your own Spirit Guides, Angels, or divinatory tools as you seek to understand the deeper mysteries of existence. The clearer your need is defined, the more articulate the question will be. The more plainly the question is stated, the greater the probability that you will be given information and answers that you can actually apply in your life. This mental and emotional clarity is vital, since the more obscure the mystery, the more profound the answer will be. When consulting the Oracle, there is a subtle warning. Unless you truly want to know, it would be wiser not to ask. More often than not, you will be given the information that you need rather than what you would like to hear. It is not the Oracle's job description to offer you tea and pat your hand while soothingly cooing, "There, there." It's an Oracle's duty to "lay the cards on the table" and give you the unvarnished truth. Oh, you can always find a self-proclaimed Seer who is happy to take your money for vague assurances, but in reality, very little is more frustrating than asking what you consider a direct question to the human form of a Magic 8 Ball and the answer is "Try again later . . . more tea?"

The Oracle dances to the music of the waves at the edge of the vast cosmic ocean. The waves rise to clothe her in gossamer as she twirls beneath the soft light of the crescent moon. Above two majestic stone pillars—one dark for chaos, and one light, representing order—the windswept clouds are illuminated against a star-filled indigo sky. Far in the distance, at the edge of the known world, stands another pair of monolithic pillars marking the distant gateway to the deeper consciousness of our psyche. The Oracle embodies the youthful Goddess, bringing forth mysteries from the unknown emotional depths of our being and into the lives of those who are willing to hear. These turbulent seas of unsettled emotions take form and purpose in the Oracle's presence. White foam adorns, softens, and defines the edges of tempestuous feelings with musings and possibilities. She brings forth the unconscious with intuitive grace and reveals the truth to all who seek wisdom as her dance flows seamlessly in the narrow chasm between chaos and order.

Guidelines: Revealing what was before unseen, hidden, and secret. If the person chooses to listen, knowledge and wisdom are being shared that will be of great value to the Seeker. The barriers between the body, mind, and spirit have been dispersed. Access to ancient truths is now granted to the Seeker. Listen carefully and stay the course.

Reversed: You're in over your head. Deception, lies, and half truths are the coin of passage for those who are attempting to cheat their way to positions of power. Redefine your questions and priorities and ask again. You are being told and shown falsehoods designed to ensnare and trap your very soul.

Notes:

4 Divine Feminine

You are a wanted
child of an abundant universe.

Inspired by the Tarot's "The Empress." The number 4 portrays a solid, steady, firm foundation.

Representing the Divine Feminine is Danu. She is personified from the collective name of the Irish gods Tuatha De Danann or "The people of the goddess Danu" and is the most ancient of the Celtic Gods. The root "dan" in ancient Irish means art, skill, poetry, knowledge, and wisdom. For many, Danu has come to represent the Earth Mother Goddess and is known for her compassion and patience in teaching her children. She also provides the raw materials to form and feed our bodies. She is the breath of life that courses through our bodies and feeds our spirits. She restores our souls when we gaze upon her majesty in the landscapes that surround and support us. Her children come in many forms. Some walk on two legs, some on four, while others navigate the waters . . . all are precious to Her.

In our lives, we may not always be able to "Honor thy Mother." But we can always honor our Earth Mother that nurtures and sustains us. We can step gently upon the earth when walking barefoot through the meadow and allow the beauty and peace to flow through and restore us. This Mother we can and should honor and care for with all of our beings. Although generous, and supportive, she is also fierce in her mandates. When she says, "Sit," your rear end had better drop into that chair . . . now. She possesses the notorious "Mom Voice" that can be heard with the heart if you're attentive enough to hear. She is ever the warrior and always your defender that will strike fear into the most stalwart adversary. Solid and grounded, this Great Mother is steady and focused. For the Divine Feminine, there is one rule: "All life is sacred." No exceptions. Because all life is sacred, it must be honored and not harmed in any way . . . unless it threatens her children. Then it's okay to kill it . . . but in reference to the One Rule, if you kill it, you have to eat it.

The Divine Feminine is the Mother aspect of the Triple Goddess. She is the one who nurtures and protects her children, as well as the warrior who defends those in her care. Surrounded by an ancient primordial forest, the Mother holds a basin overflowing with the Waters of Eternal Life. Brilliant, lavender lotus flowers bloom within the bowl's depths, symbolizing the beauty of spiritual awareness that springs from the muddy depths of our psyche. Clothed in a verdant robe, the Divine Feminine is surrounded by crimson hibiscuses, which are nourished by the life-giving waters. From the stream flowing at her feet, the Salmon of Knowledge containing all the knowledge and wisdom of the world leaps upward toward the divine source. Her voice can be heard in the wind as it whispers her song through the leaves in the trees. Her subtle creativity is often found in the lace patterns of sunlight on the ever-changing canvas of the forest floor. Her legend is told with each sigh of peace, each cry of the hawk, and the laughter of water dancing over the rocks. She is the essence of creation and wields the magic of the divine flow. From her bounty and abundance, we are born wanted children of an abundant universe.

Guidelines: Know that you are a beloved child of an ever-expanding universe. Beauty, abundance, grace, and new life are the gifts being offered to you. Now is the time to embrace all that life has to offer. Allow your inner goddess to step forth and become a beacon to reunite all parts of yourself that have been abandoned. Become your own mentor.

Reversed: The self-absorbed narcissistic personality has robbed life of all joy. The one who is meant to sustain and nurture has been depleted and has no more to give. There may be problems with one's offspring, or unplanned, unwanted pregnancy. The belief in "lack" has manifested in dark ways. Refusing to accept responsibility for the care of those in your charge will cause long-term damage if not remedied immediately. Seek counsel from your inner Crone.

Notes:

5 The Crone

The ancestral keeper of family wisdom.

The matriarch of the human tribe completes the 3 of the triple goddess. The number 5 represents feminine = chaos = expansion.

The Crone is the mature aspect of the Triple Goddess. As Matriarch of her tribe, she is the Wise Woman, the Healer who has brought forth new life in all forms for countless generations. She is the storyteller whose musings are shining, golden nuggets hiding in the rocks beneath the sparkling stream. Her apothecary is the garden behind her cottage, the flowers that adorn her walkway, and the lands surrounding her people. She knows there are no weeds, and that each plant, each bit of soil, and each stone contain health and healing for any who are in need. The Crone has lived long enough to understand she can and always will still learn but is willing to share her accumulated knowledge and experiences with those who seek her out. She is the Grandmother, ancient and wise, having been there, done that—she has the postcard and the T-shirt and is still on the mailing list.

"Listen to your elders!" These words have been spoken and repeated to every child born since the beginning. As children, we ask, "Why?" Why should we listen to the old person sitting on the porch? Youth and ambition often have little or no patience to listen to the meanderings of the elderly. It isn't until they move out into the world that they truly appreciate the value of our tribe and our village. Only when our familial safety net is missing do we fully recognize the value, comfort, and security that belonging to a community brings. There are always the ones smart enough to have paid attention to the stories and lessons. They have heeded the counsel of their elders and will step outside their boundaries with a degree of confidence. These youths are usually savvy enough to know how far and how fast to travel and how far to push the boundaries. When this happens, the Crone will modify her counsel and protection. She knows that the most-valuable lessons are not always learned in winning, and that the young ones will gain knowledge and find the beginning of wisdom when they don't succeed and things don't go as planned. As her children make their way in the world, there will be times she will simply stand by with a scoop shovel and a first-aid kit, quietly shaking her head as the child of her heart speeds swiftly and furiously into the proverbial, unyielding brick wall.

Mounted upon an ebony mare, the Crone travels through her domain. She proudly wears her silver hair and wrinkled features as badges of maturity. Clothed in a scarlet-red gown, she carries with her a silver-trimmed leather shield with the symbol of the Triskelion embossed upon its surface. In her right hand, she holds a hazel-wood wand topped by the Triquetra representing the Triple Goddess. Far away, the mountain is surrounded in mystery and myth. Nearby, an apple tree bearing fruit promises knowledge and immortality as told in the story of the famed, mystical Isle of Avalon (from the Welch word for apple, *afal*) the magical place of eternal rest for Celtic heroes. The waterfall symbolizes that harsh disappointment will make one wiser and often relates to a great release of emotion followed by the renewal of spirit. The brilliant, crimson hops' leaves promise to heal through rest and sleep.

Guidelines: Wisdom, grace, and knowledge are the fruits of a life spent in service. Having the well-being of one's family, neighbors, and community in your care is both taxing and rewarding. Be mindful of the gifts of the season and fill your larder with what life has offered. The shelters are prepared, the harvest is gathered, and the seed for next season is safely stored. Be at peace as you freely share your knowledge and wisdom. Your words do not fall on deaf ears.

Reversed: Advanced age does not always guarantee wisdom. However, wiser minds than yours are offering sage advice, and it would be in your best interest to listen. Be patient with the elderly and remember who it was that taught you to use a spoon. There may come a time when someone or something has passed its expiration date. Perhaps the elderly have become difficult and need alternative living arrangements? The decisions will either haunt you or bring peace . . . perhaps both.

Notes:

6 Elder Gods

Honoring our ancestors.

Inspired by the Tarot's "The Emperor." Number 6 brings the energy of practicality and represents the masculine principle of order.

The Elder Gods' primal male energies bring discipline and order to the unknown wilds. With principles and doctrine as hard as granite, these Gods command the primeval forest, tempestuous seas, and vast landscapes. But unlike granite, the Elder Gods can and will retaliate against those who seek to destroy their domain. For untold millennia, their stories and deeds have been passed down through the generations. Tales of heroes long buried and epic songs of glory capture our imaginings and our souls that cry out for honor, justice, and freedom.

Only by honoring all with whom we share our planet can we survive and prosper. We are not all born to lead. Soldiers, citizens, and families are also essential to the delicate ecosystem of our societies within our vast and varied civilizations. It's vital that we stay connected to our roots. Only through history can we see where our paths diverge and meet. Only by studying the past can we remember and learn from our transgressions and victories. We cannot survive by focusing on our differences. Our strength, our future depends on our common humanity. The World Tree's roots run deep and touch each and every part of existence. To deny or ignore the existence of the ancient teachings would not be unlike chopping down the World Tree for firewood. By looking only at the needs and agenda of today, the destruction would be the equivalent of building one's own funeral pyre from all that is sacred. To be given "dominion" over the earth and its inhabitants does not give one license to dominate and destroy. After all, it is unsanitary to defecate in your own backyard. Plus, you will eventually step in it . . . which is disgusting.

Before time, before history, the Elder Gods came to be in our forests, waters, and mountains. They brought order to chaos and charmed beasts with their music, words, and presence. These gods were a part of, rather than apart from, those wild passions we are taught to fear and deny. Here is the Grand Father, the one whose body is the trunk, branches, and roots of the ancient trees, and his bones the granite of the earth. His hair is wild winter snow, and stone becomes his skin. The tattoo on his arm honors the dragon, which symbolizes courage and great power. Since dragons protect the Earth and all living things, they are considered the most powerful of all the Celtic symbols. The golden armband denotes the masculine attributes of protection, growth, and knowledge. His leather vest is adorned with golden symbols of eternal divinity. From his belt hangs a hunting horn. Since horns are an animal's weapon, it follows that they serve as a symbol representing strength and aggression. They also symbolize the power and dignity of divinity, as his horned headdress declares him the Lord of Animals. His staff of yew denotes his dominion over all that is primal and raw. The Stag signals that the time has come for a quest, and announces the God's arrival in the misty forest. First, the Elder God masters himself. For what is true mastery without first being whole? He leads by example in the old ways, walking the old path.

Guidelines: Strength and honor are the foundations of peace and freedom. To be strong and fierce in the face of adversity, to gain victory against overwhelming odds, these are the fires that feed the soul's forge. To protect those who are vulnerable is the highest calling for those who seek to be of service. Solid and steady, the forces that govern the wilderness must first master their own inner beast.

Reversed: There is a clear and present danger of being overwhelmed by forces beyond your control. The ground beneath you is not bedrock, but shifting sands that will swallow you and your army. Be aware of the enemy at the gate. You have been deceived and outmaneuvered. The true enemy remains strong. Now is not the time to pursue victory. You need to gather your forces and organize your assets.

Notes:

7 Tradition

When the student is ready, the master appears.

Inspired by the Tarot's "The Hierophant." Number 7 is the number of magic, wisdom, and study.

From generation to generation we pass down the knowledge, wisdom, and traditions of our tribes. Our community is thus preserved and strengthened by its common core beliefs and practices. We may vary greatly in physical appearance, personal taste, and preferences, but we come together bringing our commonalities under one banner to form our villages, towns, cities, and countries. Traditions are the glue that binds us together, as well as the container that holds us as it establishes our core identity and values. When we gather to celebrate, mourn, or learn, the customs and culture of our tribe dictate the proceedings for each event. Often, as we expand and evolve, and if we're lucky, others come and bring new traditions to complement those that exist. As we nourish our bodies with food, so do new traditions from other cultures find their way into our communal stews. They bring exotic spices, new flavors, and exciting blends of culinary delights in food for our tables, styles of dress, and exhilarating dance, to name just a few. The community at large will choose which new traditions to add to their customs. Much like new recipes, what may sound good doesn't always blend well. Which is why adding raisins to meatloaf has never been popular. This is how we evolve as a community.

"It takes a village" is one of the truisms that are as valid today as it has been since the forming of family and communal groups. Each member brings something of value to the table. Old or young, we owe it to our communities to share experience, knowledge, and wisdom. Although change is inevitable lest atrophy rule, changes must also be made on solid desire to create stable abundance for the greater good. Thus traditions, old and new, must be honored and wedded together in a cohesive and timely manner to be taught both at home and in institutions to the new generation. For example, a time-honored tradition of honoring the elders and heeding their wisdom has sadly diminished. Through their long lives and vast experience, elders traditionally held a place of respect in communities and served as the shaman, knowledge keepers, religious leaders, and shapers of community standards. Today, these roles have weakened as consumerism and our myopic celebration of youth, along with the rejections of tradition, have spread across the globe. Recognizing the limitless value of elders and taking advantage of all the knowledge they possess can be an important tool in cultivating today's traditions that reinforce sustainable practices.

Beneath a star-filled indigo sky, the Shaman passes on the illuminated knowledge of the tribe to the acolytes. Garbed in the blue of mastery, the Teacher illustrates the value of symbols and their meanings to the young ones. A raven comes to land on his shoulder, bringing yet more messages from the gods. While beneath the branches of the sacred ash tree, robed in the browns of raw earth colors, one acolyte keeps tempo on a rawhide drum decorated with the sacred dragon totem while the other utilizes an amethyst pendulum to enhance clarity. Both the dragon and the owl symbolize wisdom to aid the apprentices in learning the traditions of their people.

Guidelines: Finding comfort in community and established customs. Dancing to a familiar song with a partner you've long been acquainted with. Peace and tranquility are found in time-honored rituals. The student is called to seek the master. The master adds to his existing knowledge when a brilliant apprentice finds a new way. Knowledge is gained from a reliable, familiar source.

Reversed: What has worked before needs adapting. In other words, just because your father and your grandfather did it that way doesn't mean it's the right or proper way. Which begs the question "How did that work out for them?" Blindly following the custom will not serve you or the community. Find another path. Dance to your own drummer. There is a vast difference between keeping with tradition and being too lazy to find a better way forward.

Notes:

8 Choices

Define what is sacred and that which is profane.

Inspired by the Tarot's "The Lovers." Number 8 unites the material and the spiritual.

A fundamental aspect of choice is between what is sacred and what is profane. If you have to ask, "Is this ethical?," the answer is probably "No." The choice is also Free Will. We are always free to choose. If someone cries, "I had no choice!," they are sadly mistaken. There is always a choice. You may not like the choices, but they're still valid. If the decision is the choice between bodily harm, dire circumstances, or even death, then what must be examined are the millions, or more, moment-to-moment decisions that brought about these do-or-die circumstances. It's rarely one monumental choice that backs a person into a corner. Do you choose your lovers, friends, and companions on the basis of clear sight and compatibility? Or are you terrified of being alone and choose from desperation? Do you see a potential mate and think, "There's a real fixer-upper!"? Do you find yourself repeating patterns of destructive relationships where each time you believe this is the one? Eye colors may differ, as do hair colors and other unimportant attributes, but the core personality and consequential outcome continue to remain constant in every relationship. To word it differently, what compels you to make the choices you make? By objectively examining our choices we will reveal the patterns that have become ingrained in our psyches. When we learn to identify and opt out of destructive patterns, our choices will naturally become more productive and beneficial.

When choosing friends, companions, or mates, too often we seek someone we believe will complete us. The irony here lies in the truth that we are already whole and complete unto ourselves. There may be parts that have been injured or damaged during our lives, which we have carefully wrapped in cotton batting and tucked away in a safe place with the promise of "I'll be back for you later." The problem is that every time you reexamine that injury, all the emotional trauma associated with the event strikes with the subtlety of a tsunami. We are immediately overwhelmed and naturally run away once again, leaving the broken pieces of ourselves behind. However, what if you talk to yourself then as you are now? Why not approach the wounded inner child as the parent, teacher, or mentor you have become? First, know that the choices the other you made were done with all the intelligence, experience, and wisdom you possessed at that time. Even if you did nothing, that was a choice. But now, as an older, wiser you, you can counsel the younger you with compassion. You can become your own Spirit Guide and recover the missing parts with gentle strength and love, thus moving forward toward wholeness.

Her golden cup overflows with both purity of spirit and carnal desire. The Serpent of Wisdom that twines around her body is echoed in the stem of the illuminated chalice. White, translucent orbs surround the Cup Bearer, providing protection and undesignated energies that ensure the purity of intent. Dual forces emanate from the cup to flow and surround those seeking her affections and attention. Those who cling to her offer either temptation and unbridled passion or security and steadfast devotion. One offers order, safety, and complete comfort. The other promises chaos, uncertainty, and sensual passion. It is up to you to choose.

Guidelines: The more closely we choose to align with Spirit, the closer we get to achieving wholeness. The choice here is between what is sacred to you and what you believe to be profane. Listen closely to what your heart is saying. Ask the person you will be tomorrow how this decision tastes the morning after. Where does this choice lead you in three days, months, or years? Gather your knowledge, experience, and wisdom to make the best choice possible for you and you alone.

Reversed: A relationship is in danger of being lost or broken. Trust is being destroyed by an ill-considered decision. There is the possibility of indiscretion and infidelity. There is no honor in being indecisive. The answer is not in the guise of others. The flimsy excuse "The Devil made me do it" doesn't let you off the hook for the choices made. Ignoring the situation will not make it go away. Remember that your most important relationship is with yourself. A choice must be made.

Notes:

9 Sacred Alignment

Opposing forces are focused on a common goal.

Inspired by the Tarot's "The Chariot." Number 9 is the path toward mystical knowledge.

Often in our journey through life, we encounter forces far beyond our control. These forces, either by chance or design, are more often than not there for our mutual benefit. If we learn to relinquish control and allow the energies to carry us forward, we will travel in comfort and always arrive at the next destination either at or ahead of the appointed time. To summarize, sit down and fasten your seat belt. Keep your hands and feet inside the vehicle at all times. Under no circumstances should you stand up until the ride has come to a complete halt. The beauty of Sacred Alignment is much like taking the train or a bus. Just find your seat and enjoy the scenery. Actually, there are not many other options, due to the fact the forces at work here are far, far beyond anything we, as mere mortals, can direct. And for the record, it can and often does rival Mr. Toad's Wild Ride at Disneyland.

    It is somewhat terrifying knowing that the energies at work are exact polar opposites and function much like magnets. If you've ever taken a small but powerful magnet and tried to force the positive ends together, you have a general idea of these energies. These are natural forces that have been drawn into synchronicity in order to achieve that perfect union between chaos and order. This is the equivalent of traversing that thin line between chaos and order, which is always in flux and akin to the yin-yang symbol. By maintaining balance, you have arrived at that sweet spot known in ancient Greek philosophy, particularly that of Aristotle, as the golden mean or golden middle way. This describes the desirable middle way between two extremes, one of excess and the other of deficiency, also described as "virtue" in his writing. Once achieved and maintained, it allows the traveler to flow seamlessly from one part of the journey to the next.

    The Master Wizard stands balanced astride two magnificent Friesian warhorses. Strong winds whip his long, snow-white hair and beard into wildness while twisting the manes and tails of his mounts into fairy braids as they charge with fierce determination through the gathering mists. Upon his brow rests a platinum-winged band to augment his spiritual strength and stability. Centered between the wings is an oval-shaped chevron amethyst to promote calm, balanced peace, and patience. This stone also assists in enhancing intuition and is a powerful force for dissipating and repelling negativity. His dark, flowing gray robes denote his neutrality in all judgments and affairs. The Master carries a staff of ash wood, whose properties include balance and the marriage of opposites. A living star atop the staff streams runes of light named Laguz for flow, Ehwaz for movement, and Raido for travel. From time immemorial, horses bring freedom, power, and majesty to the journey. A black steed represents mystery, death, and rebirth and requires a leap of faith. The white symbolizes mastery of knowledge, faith, spiritual progress, and reason. Together they form a powerful union signifying true power in the wisdom found in remembering your journey as a whole.

Guidelines: Bound by a common goal, the Sacred Alignment navigates the currents and eddies to travel in safety to the next destination. Your journey has begun anew. Trust in the forces that govern the Universe to ensure your safe travels and arrivals. Any conflicts will be surmounted and overcome, with victory ensured. Align your desire with Divine Will to achieve your goals.

Reversed: Rules are simple and easy to follow, except for those who have what are known as "control issues." Here is where you might want to check your map and stop thinking you know where you are going. You do not know. Your energies are scattered in the manner of a shotgun. In order to move ahead, you need to refocus your energy into a laser-like beam. It is okay to get lost. It is foolish to stay lost.

Notes:

10 Soul Fire

Define the source of your personal power.

Inspired by the Tarot's "Strength." Number 10 finds completeness in divine order.

From what source do you find strength? Is it the love of power that drives you onward toward greatness? Or is it the power of love that kindles the fire in your spirit? When you have explored the motivation behind your actions, eventually you find a still point where burns a single flame. What do you feed your inner fire? When your energies are depleted and taking another step would require a Herculean effort, what makes you find the inner fortitude to take that step and all the steps that follow? Ask yourself: Is it the cry of a child, the cry of battle, or the cry of anger that instills determination and a sense of purpose in you? Whatever makes you move, feel, and act is what is feeding the soul's fire within you. By searching within, you may find there are multiple types of fuel that feed these flames of passion, desire, and resolve. The inner voice may first whisper, "Maybe I can?," but the more you fan the flames, the stronger the voice becomes until you rise in passion and glory to shout, "Yes! I can!" Or at the very least nod knowingly with a Mona Lisa smile and go forth to conquer both your inner demons and a few notable adversaries.

We each have a hidden well of strength, stamina, and fortitude. The idea is not only to find that hidden source but to learn to draw from it when needed. From the exhausted single parent who sits up all night with a sick child to the battle-hardened warrior who braves enemy fire to save a friend, strength is taking that one deep breath and putting one's self forward. It is digging deep and scraping away false notions and others' opinions that have been given to you as truths. It is thinking you have hit rock bottom only to have your toddler walk into the room needing to be saved because there are monsters under the bed. No matter how exhausted, the parent will don their mental armor, arm themselves with wooden spoons and spatulas, and vanquish the vicious beast from under the child's bed, never to return, once more ensuring safety in the kingdom. Or perhaps it is the stranger who rushes toward the explosion to help those who may be victims of violence, with no thought for their own safety. When one's soul fires burn brightly, if the fuel that feeds the flames is pure, we become everyday heroes to those we cherish.

As the sun sets on a crisp autumn evening, the Forester rests on a time-worn tree stump. Surrounded by the ancient woodland, she is dressed in furs and animal hides found abandoned by those who no longer have need of physical form or warmth. Sheltered beneath a primordial alder tree, she holds a staff gifted to her by the ancient tree. The staff is crowned by living flame fed by Divine Spirit. A winter-white bear cub tucks its head beneath her hand in a gesture of trust and friendship, while a night-black cub stretches up to put its paws on her outstretched leg, seeking her attention. At this moment all fear is released. Here we find our courage and our true strength.

Guidelines: Courage isn't the absence of fear. Courage comes when the fear is acknowledged and accepted, and then you choose to proceed in the face of that fear. Strength isn't always about a test of arms or who can win the battle. Strength is about what motivates you to test or to fight. Look within, dig deeper than you have ever searched to find the wellspring of strength that is yours and yours alone.

Reversed: You must find a way to renounce all fear. The wild forces within, when not properly monitored and maintained, can ignite and burn out of control, consuming you and all that surrounds you in blinding fires of hatred. You must ask yourself: Does the love of power or the power of love define me? Seek to understand what feeds your Soul's Fire. Although we may be as hard as stone, we are not stone. Stone never retaliates.

Notes:

11 Spirit Guide

Let your inner light become a beacon in the darkness.

Inspired by the Tarot's "The Hermit," the number 11 brings higher intuition and spiritual insight.

As twilight settles over the timberland, ethereal mists gather, bringing both peace and mystery. The forest becomes a place of magical enchantment. Soft indigos color the surrounding landscape in hues and shades representing mastery and spirit. In the times of dawn and dusk, the barriers dissolve and the way between the worlds opens for travelers. In these times and places, we find our guides, mentors, ancestors, and totems waiting to bring knowledge, share wisdom, and offer guidance. It is primordial human nature to fear the darkness of the unknown, but these times between are more likely to fill us with invigorating excitement as we breathe in the formless possibilities of the eternal spirit. It is also in our nature as humans to seek light in the darkness, for even the light of a single candle can show the way to comfort and safety. But the time of the half light can and does offer a sense of peace in and of itself. In between the day and the night exist a solitude that carries solace and security that permeates one's entire being. This is accompanied by an inner knowing that being alone and loneliness are exclusive states of being. Here resides "Being" in its truest form. Here you learn to be alone.

The wisest, most-profound answers are always found within. At times we need to withdraw from society, forgo the social gatherings, and spend time with our own inner guidance. This is important because without spending good-quality time with yourself, you will never know who you truly are capable of becoming. Too often we let the opinions and judgments of others define us. Only in solitude will we find that which we seek. Meditation, prayer, and quiet contemplation are the gateways to communicate with what guides us. For what we seek is not "out there" but can be found only within. By turning inward we seek and find the true light of our own being. It begins as a spark and blossoms into a brilliant light to guide you from the dark night of the soul to the brilliance of a shining star. You become the light in the dark.

The wizened master lifts his lantern in search of lost souls. The stained-glass lantern's panels depict oak leaves, representing strength. The lamp's copper metal frame conducts spiritual energies between the material plane and other dimensions. Robed in an earth-colored garment, his loyalty, common sense, and devotion are paralleled with a great sense of duty and responsibility. His staff of beechwood bears a rare amethyst, whose royal-purple color acts as a spiritual shield while protecting against lower energies. The crystal's unique double-terminated base of iridescent emerald green promotes healing and a sense of well-being. The master's belt holds a bag of herbs and stones. It is decorated with a crow's feather for assistance in receiving messages from the gods, a key to symbolize his ability to unlock the secrets of the unknown; a bear's claw brings gentle spiritual strength, and a golden-orange maple leaf signifies unity and peace. The bag is also adorned with turquoise, which brings wisdom and spiritual grounding, as well as coral for protection against evil, malachite for spiritual healing, and abalone shell for emotional balance and tranquility.

Guidelines: Now is the time to become a beacon of spirit. When you find yourself alone in the dark, breathe life into your Spirit and allow your Light to shine. Know that you are never truly alone. Spend time with your inner guides, mentors, ancestors, and animal totems. Integrate all parts of your innermost being into a single, bright star of light to guide others safely into the harbor.

Reversed: It is when we seek to validate ourselves by obtaining the approval of others that we are doomed to believe we are complete failures. No amount of money, time, or effort will ever compensate for what is true and desperately needed. We may even pray for divine guidance, beseeching our god or goddess to intervene on our behalf, only to have our prayers fall on deaf ears. Seek guidance from within, not without.

Notes:

12 Wheel of Time

The present moment contains the whole of existence.

Inspired by the Tarot's "The Wheel of Fortune," the number 12 represents a completed cycle of experience.

In recent decades, "Time" has been viewed by many in the metaphysical field as the ever-present moment, or the "Now." Whether we view time as a temporal passage or "becoming" and "progressing," we still live within certain constraints and laws. Whichever way time is viewed, "Now" is and will always be our starting point. It is our perception of time that keeps everything from happening at once, so we can truly savor, or abhor, the current experience. To take this one step beyond, we can observe the past, apply the current knowledge we have, and perhaps steer ourselves to safety, so as not to let the wheel of time flatten us into the mud. The moment-to-moment flashes segue into the illusion of flow. This perception of time can be experienced as shooting the rapids down a treacherous mountain gorge or lazily allowing the currents and eddies to move you gradually down the stream as you idly try to figure out what pictures you're seeing in the clouds. Either way, you might want to dress appropriately or pack an umbrella, because eventually you're going to get soaked. Time and water are funny like that.

But for our purposes, we consider the idea of Time and existence being, for all intents and purposes, cyclic. From birth to death to the wheel of Karma and reincarnation, the Wheel of Time's spin is one of our perceived constants. The wheel can represent cycles of life, seasons, or reincarnation, depending on your beliefs. What originally began as a tool for creation (as in the first wheel was for pottery) eventually, in roughly 300 years, became adapted to use in chariots for transportation. There is no "wheel" in nature. It is one of the few, rare 100% inventions of humankind. The wheel, which the goddess Fortuna spins to determine the fate of those she looks upon, is, depending on which academic you consult, an ancient concept of either Greek or Roman origin. Regardless, the concept caught on quickly and has been adapted for use in cultures around the globe.

The four fixed signs of the zodiac frame the Wheel of Time while nesting in a field of stars against an indigo sky. To begin, the sign of Aquarius heralds the age in which we live. The sign of the Water Bearer brings a social conscience to the era and represents the element of air. Next in the heavens is Scorpio. With deep sensitivity, this sign brings concern for beginnings and endings, without fear of either, to portray the element of water. The sign of Leo, from the constellation of the same name, brings qualities of leadership, a sense of pride, and an air of royalty, while adding the element of fire. Taurus contributes physical pleasure, material goods, and the enjoyment of tactile experiences to the mix, along with the element of earth. The hourglass represents balance and equilibrium, with the upper part always being "heaven" and the lower representing "earth." These seven star-filled crystal hourglasses interlock to form the celestial wheel. As the great wheel turns, we are reminded that the sands of time slip by with or without our attention or permission. Ever changing, in constant motion, the Wheel of Time assures us that nothing is truly here to stay and that this too shall pass.

Guidelines: Changes are upon you. Allow yourself to move through each moment by breathing in its essence. As each moment is received, consider its value without prejudice or judgment. Observe the ebb and flow around you as you maintain your still point at the center of the Great Wheel. Stand firm at this moment as the sands of time flow endlessly around you.

Reversed: You cannot push the river, nor can you speed or slow time. Only by embracing each moment of "now" will you find the courage and strength to endure. It seems that the universe has conspired against you and that disappointment, sadness, and loss dominate your life. Remember, this is a coming to be and a passing away, not that which abides. Do not let this experience define you.

Notes:

13 The Law

The law is for all.

Inspired by the Tarot's "Justice," the number 13 represents karma.

The law applies to the highest and the lowest. It is for all, and there are none above or outside the law. The Law is unbiased, balanced, and impersonal. It cares not for beauty or riches but is founded on giving. As the proverb "A gift demands a gift" reads, so does the law determine your worth. Yet, this law cannot be bought or sold. It is unbreakable, secure, and immutable. It is the Law of Spirit and supersedes the laws of man, religions, ideologies, and governments. There is no escape from Spiritual Law. It is handed down by Divine Providence to each and every being. There is no bartering with this law. Knowing that this fundamental, core truth is at the center of humanity's soul should be binding us together as opposed to driving wedges between us. It has been spoken or written in all languages known to man, and a few others we are still trying to decipher. It is what constitutes each person's moral fiber.

To clarify, throughout history each culture has voiced the law and passed it along to others. The biblical law reads "You reap as you sow" and is repeated in the Law of Karma, to name two instances. But what about times of war, when it is imperative that each side believes in their divine right to dominate and rule? How are we to fathom who is right and who is not, since the victors write the histories? Luckily, we don't have to decide anything. This decision is between the individual, their personal deity, and their beliefs. At this juncture of life passing into death, many cultures believe in an afterlife where they are judged by their Creator for their worth. At the end of the current life, each being will then be granted the grand prize of a glorious afterlife or condemned to the pits of damnation for eternity . . . unless they have a "Get out of jail free" card that may be used at this time. This is otherwise known as moral-justice "points," which can be acquired through good deeds and acts of kindness.

A snow-covered mountain dominates the background. Golden twin pillars and a silver ceiling grace the shining domain of justice and mediation. This court is known by all who come before the arbiter as a place of justice and reconciliation. His ax represents the power of destruction and creation and can often be found in the hands of a Gnostic warrior. It is both a weapon and a tool, portraying the duality and balanced purpose of the law. His robe, fashioned from a grizzly bear's discarded form, denotes strength and inner wisdom. Wearing a kilt made from gray wolf fur symbolizes neutrality in social issues. He sits upon a marble chair. The back of his seat is inlaid with sacred cedar, which forms the Celtic symbol for Justice. His gold armband and breastplate signify the right to pass judgment. He listens without bias or prejudice. He sees with clarity and knows the truth of the petitioner's heart. The Universe has heard and reviewed your petition. Your choices have brought you here and now.

Guidelines: You are receiving the proportion of equal amounts, that which you have put into a project, an investment, or your life. The rewards and accolades awarded you are the proper payment for the efforts you have extended. The decision is just and has been made in fairness. You have been granted what is your due, and now it is up to you to gather your resources and achieve your goals.

Reversed: "There ain't any free lunch." More effort is needed from you or on your behalf in order to gain what you believe is rightfully yours. Lack of accountability has led to dishonesty, flaws, and legal complications. It is in your best interest to find where the system has failed, and then take steps to correct the errors. No one can do this for you. The next step is entirely up to you.

Notes:

14 Perception

Explore other avenues.

Inspired by the Tarot's the "Hanged Man," number 14 adequately perceives any situation.

Between our commitments to allow events to unfold organically and the desire to consider the individual puzzle pieces and understand what is going on, there lies the annoying idea of perception. Think of it as a mental speed bump that will take out the undercarriage of your vehicle if you don't notice it and slow down. What seems like a colossal roadblock may, in reality, be only a slight course change. What you experience emotionally truly does depend on your personal viewpoint. When confronted with the big, scary monster that is usually safely tucked under the bed or locked in the closet, the wisest decision would be to stop and choose a course of action before proceeding. By taking a mental half step sideways, backing up a bit, and gaining another point of view we often find that what we believed to be a major problem is nothing more than a slight inconvenience. Whoever or whatever has your attention and might be consuming your thoughts and energy and diverting you from your goal. So ask yourself, "Is it worthy of my consideration?"

However, from another perspective, there are often times when the need to put ourselves in another's position and experience the events from their point of view is paramount. What motivates one person to greatness may inspire only mediocrity in another. All in all, it is the relevance and importance we assign to the motivating factor that either builds a fire under us or douses the flame. Which is why taking the opportunity to view the situation from another perspective can be both educational and informative. Then, and only then, may we understand the significance between allowing things to take their natural course and trimming the sails on the boat to adjust our course. The ultimate goal here is to recognize established patterns of behavior. Some serve you well and therefore will continue to be used. Others have long since outworn their usefulness and need to be assigned to the recycle bin. How well this works will depend on how willing you are to let go of what no longer serves. Recognition is a key factor here. If it's not broken, don't fix it. If it is broken, how bad is the damage? Is it a "duct tape and hammer" kind of repair job? Or does this require surgical skills to remove the blight from existence? Once you have observed the person or situation from all angles, the answer will be clear. Then allow the natural selection process to begin. You've got this.

Cumulus clouds swirl across a cobalt-verdant Earth as it hangs in a star-filled sky. Swirls of stardust glitter in brilliant contrast to the eternal cerulean blue of beyond. On the luminous rocky surface of the moon, a sapphire-blue dragon rests comfortably with his person. The dragon's gleaming golden crest and wings reflect the light of the hidden sun. His ivory horns defend the one in his charge from harm. Upon his leg, he cradles a raven-haired maiden as she rests her head against his smooth, scaled face. Dressed in gossamer white, with her feet tucked under her gown, her arms gently cradle her knees as she gazes at the Earth in quiet contemplation. In silent companionship, millions of miles away from here and now, they each reflect inward toward their own perception.

Guidelines: Total and complete understanding allows you to let it be without judgment or prejudice. Surrendering to the Higher Authority that dwells within brings clarity of thought and purpose. Gaining a different perspective brings an enlightened perception of the person, situation, and events. You may see things more clearly when you look with more than your eyes.

Reversed: How can you expect others to afford you the opportunity to change when you are not allowing it for yourself? Old ideas, views, and values no longer serve who you are now. You need a different perspective if you are going to alter your perception. Look at what surrounds you and see what makes your teeth itch, and then take the necessary steps to correct the situation.

Notes:

15 The Traveler

The new life is always greater than the old.

Inspired by the Tarot's "Death," the number 15 represents a synthesis of spirit and matter.

With transformation comes change. When the time comes, we metaphorically mimic the butterfly and cocoon ourselves in bindings of our own making and design to secure a place for personal transformations to occur. Eventually, we emerge from a closed, chrysalis state into that which we are destined to become. From that moment, we embrace the Art of Being and live our lives authentically with purpose and dedication. Or at least that's the plan. But we have all learned that while we go about our busy lives making plans, the gods and goddesses laugh and laugh. There are few, if any, eureka moments when we magically transition into a state of grace. Instead, we accept the role of the traveler, placing one foot in front of the other as we journey through this lifetime. With time, knowledge, and a bit of wisdom, we go beyond acceptance and actively embrace each moment of our journey. By now we have learned it's the journey that matters as much or more than the arrival at a given destination. Even stepping off the boat or a plane on your dream vacation of a lifetime puts your feet firmly on the path of discovery. At least one hopes you don't stay at the airport or the dock for the allotted time, blissfully unaware there is more to see and experience just beyond the door.

Additionally, embracing the concept of life being a journey and you being a traveler takes a bit of the pressure off. When viewing situations and circumstances as signposts, and other people as fellow travelers, your perspective shifts. From here you no longer feel the need to reach some unseen, often-fabricated goal. Instead, as travelers, we find the willingness to accept personal responsibility on the journey through self-awareness. We also accept and understand that the only constant is change itself. Without change, we suffer stagnation, which some beliefs claim to be far worse than death. For even death brings change. For instance, when a tree dies in the forest, it is reabsorbed into its surroundings, providing sustenance to the new life that springs from its fallen form. Perhaps parts of the tree will be chopped into firewood for the burning logs to provide light, heat, and comfort during times of darkness. Even ashes from the firewood have many beneficial uses. This demonstrates how each traveler, each step of the journey, and each stage of transformation add to the collective whole in all its forms.

A lone warrior stands as a sentinel on a cliff high above the indigo-blue ocean. His bow has fulfilled its purpose and now rests at his side, having guided the flaming arrows toward their goal. Gazing seaward, he watches the blazing ship as it sails purposefully toward the distant horizon. A pair of ravens named Hugin (thought) and Munin (memory) launch into the night air, winging toward the fiery beacon. They are the messengers that will carry the word of the fallen to the hall of the ancestors. As if the command were given, the flames rise up, reaching toward the stars. Dancing, transforming, and challenging the darkness, the fire transforms into a towering phoenix promising resurrection, change, and eternal life.

Guidelines: As you journey from birth to death, you will find life is a journey of discovery. Each transformation, each change, every choice is, in essence, a type of death. Whether it is a different location or a new belief, the old must move aside to make way for the new. It is within each of us to moderate, alter, and evolve beyond our current form and ideology. We must embrace all we can be, even at the risk of losing who we are.

Reversed: Refusing to move, grow, and evolve does not keep you safe. If no risks are taken, no progress can be made. Hanging on to the past stunts the growth of the person and causes stagnation in regard to the circumstances surrounding the issue. Delaying the inevitable will not benefit anyone and may cause depression. Resistance is futile and could lead to negative long-term repercussions. Do not let fear hold you back from accepting the wonderful new opportunity.

Notes:

16 Harmony

As above, so below.

Inspired by the Tarot's "Temperance, number 16 represents spiritual and analytical introspection.

The balance between the body and the soul is reflected in the inner and outer life of the individual. When ego, self, or the material desires dictate a person's choices, the soul, or the inner life, is generally hungry if not starving. This is often the case if you have chosen to feed your physical body to extremes. Be it exclusively Twinkies and soft drinks or kale and bottled water, the fuel that you put into your body will eventually overload for good or ill and hit a breaking point. When this happens, your health suffers and the Twinkie will be replaced with kale or vice versa. We know the downside of eating too much food we know isn't good for us, but we must also be aware that "too much if a good thing" is also not recommended. Not that anyone's recommending that a Twinkie a day keeps the holistic practitioner away, but there is a nutritional balance involved we must honor and adhere to in order to maintain physical health. Just as we are multidimensional beings, so our healthcare must be many faceted as well.

For example, if I'm crossing the street and get hit by a truck, I do not immediately want a Reiki master and a cup of comfrey tea. At that particular moment, I'd prefer a dose of morphine and an ambulance. After the crisis, the Reiki master and the tea would be great. To put it simply, you need balance to maintain physical health. Consequently, your body and soul also need to maintain balance, one with the other. If your soul becomes too well fed, you will for all intents and purposes be too spiritually fat to fly. If it is undernourished, it may become so weightless you will need to tie a brick around it to keep it from floating off into the void. Therefore moderation is advised. But even moderation must be used in moderation. Confused? Don't be. It's a repeated theme we find in our Journey. Walking the middle path, or following the thin line between the yin and the yang happens more easily when we avoid extremes and stay centered and calm. No, it's not always possible . . . or is it? When we maintain a healthy give and take between the physical and spiritual bodies, the flow is seamless and uninterrupted and balance is maintained.

An angelic being bridges the two halves of the wilderness landscape. Her ivory wings spread wide as she gently invites the divine light of spirit into her world. Her lap forms the lake into which authentic emotion flows from the crown of her head, creating tresses of sparkling water to cascade down her body until overflowing her crossed legs to form the rivers that nourish the land. Her arms stretched upward, hands held high, with her palms together in gratitude for the blessings bestowed from the brilliant crystalline light of spirit. In the distant horizon lie the misty forest and her ancient home. She shows the way to restore harmony between the heavens and earth that healing may be completed and all may prosper.

Guidelines: An alchemical moment when the material and the spiritual blend into something greater than the whole of the individual parts. The outer life is a reflection of the inner life and vice versa. Seeking divine intervention will lead you within to find balance and make peace with your truest self, your own divine essence. Maintaining harmony in the midst of change will strengthen your resolve and bring you the peace you desire.

Reversed: There seems to be a hole in your spiritual cup where the blessings are being poured out onto the infertile ground. If you yearn for peace, harmony, and balance you may want to do a bit of metaphysical house cleaning. The discord may be from an imbalance in a relationship, perhaps with another or with you. Are you starving your soul while enabling another to gorge? Your best support group begins with you supporting you.

Notes:

17 Attachments

Release what no longer serves who you are now.

Inspired by the Tarot's "The Devil," number 17's biblical meaning is "overcoming the enemy."

At different times in our journeys, we become inspired to explore, experience, and expand. Be it making your mark in business, art, or any other endeavor, very few are content to simply exist from birth to death. We may refer to "being called" to embark upon a certain path. When those moments happen, we feel inspired, excited, and unstoppable. Then, for a variety of reasons, "life" happens and we lose momentum. We might get stuck doing a job we despise just to pay the bills. Either way, it is not easy to avoid pitfalls and traps. This often involves the stories we tell ourselves. "I'm doing this only until I get my big break" or any number of variations along that theme are often what we sell ourselves, only to eventually become disillusioned and angry at the whole affair. This is where we learn "The Blame Game," which is itself a deadly trap. Often we have heard ourselves or someone else say, "I'd have been _____ if _____ hadn't happened," and shift the blame from where it belongs to something, somewhere, or someone else. This is the best, fastest way to metaphorically shoot yourself in the foot. The most disempowering thing we can tell ourselves is "It's not my fault!" Of course, we all have help getting there. But every time we choose victimhood over personal power, we deny our true potential. Hence, we deny our mastery.

There were certain phrases and words I did not allow my children to utter while growing up. One such phrase was "I can't because . . ." Excuses are not acceptable arguments. The bottom line is, you are the only thing in this entire universe that's strong enough to take you down. That's it. You're it. If this doesn't resonate with what you are feeling, remember how many billions of times you gave away your power. You settled, let someone else decide, or caved more than you stood your ground. Yes, there is a shadow side to this inner warrior that you've been keeping chained in your basement. There is the chance that a warrior will become a full-blown bully. But think—perhaps that's why you've experienced victimhood and now understand fully and completely who you are not. You not only know you can reclaim your power, but you understand how that power can be abused. See? It was all for a good cause.

Trapped in eternal flames of unbridled passion and hatred, a magnificent white Pegasus spreads its powerful wings. For countless ages, the depths of depression and defeat have twisted and wound its way into the once-bright spirit of the immortal winged horse. There is no savior coming to aid the fallen. There is only one way to break free of the binding captivity. Gathering inner strength, the embattled steed launches into the fiery air, knowing the inferno cannot defeat the power of the true spirit. Breaking free of the ties that bound it to the depths of hell, the Pegasus begins to take flight and reclaim the birthright of personal power.

Guidelines: Material comfort and physical pleasure may not be in your best interest. You are getting too comfortable in an assigned role that does not align with your true nature. Being seduced by the promise of luxury and power will be your downfall. Stay true to yourself and reaffirm your personal power or be prepared to suffer the consequences. It is time to take back your power.

Reversed: Free yourself from the chains of bondage. Be it physical, mental, or spiritual, those ties and obligations are not yours to bear, no matter what you have been led to believe. Replace old, harmful habits with ones that heal and protect you. Pay close attention to your inner dialogue to see what you have been programming into your beliefs and behaviors. Ignore the false evidence that appears real.

Notes:

18 Chaos

Find solace within the eye of the storm.

Inspired by the Tarot's "The Tower," number 18's underlying essence is the welfare of humanity.

If Hollywood has a motto, it's "Build a model and blow it up." At least that's the common theme if you're a fan of action movies. The Universe, on the other hand, is usually a bit more subtle. Oh, have no doubt there will still be bedlam and bulldozers resulting in a complete leveling of the playing field, but as often as not it comes as silent thunder. All you feel is a massive "WHUMP," and just like magic, the once-rock-solid whatever-it-was is gone. And don't try telling yourself these things come without warning. There are always plenty of sirens, flashing lights, and tinfoil hats to be found if you happen to be paying attention. We are not talking about watching newscasts or reading blogs. We are referring to that silent sensation right before a tornado touches down or a hurricane makes landfall. That suspended moment when there is not a breath of air, nor is there a single insect buzzing about, and all the birds have suddenly become pedestrians. Yes, those moments when something deep and primal screeches "RUN" and your lizard brain inspires you to duck for cover. Moments later, as you high-step rapidly trying to stay ahead of the tsunami or the avalanche, you're too busy running away or running toward the chaos, which generally prohibits actual thinking. In other words, you react. How you react will determine, to a considerable degree, the outcome of the ensuing chaos.

Up until the moment chaos strikes, numerous opportunities were presented to alter the present course. It generally starts small, and usually more than a few days or weeks have passed since the first warning flare went up. But it does happen. As time marches on, more and more signs come up. If they are ignored, the balance between order and chaos begins to tilt. Sooner or later the tipping point is reached, and as we watch in silent horror (or glee), the large woman in the horned helmet and brass bra is belting out the final chorus for our musical enjoyment . . . just before the curtain falls. These are the moments that define us as human beings. When the unthinkable happens, do we run away in panic or gather what we might need and hurry toward the devastation to see what we can do to help? Are we gnashing our teeth, tearing out our hair, and screaming at the heavens in impotent rage? Or do we roll up our sleeves, grab a rake, and start to work?

A cold, gray marble colossus dominates the entrance to the harbor. Posed with his arm raised to the sky, head lifted as if searching for answers to questions unasked, the once-proud symbol of a great nation stands atop a marble base where ships throughout history sought safe harbor for thousands upon thousands of years. Storm clouds boil in the heavens as lightning pierces the air with electric brilliance, illuminating the destruction of the mighty monument. Waves surge up the stone base, reaching for the chance to topple the giant effigy. The once-proud monument will soon be reduced to rubble suitable only to fill the crevices and valleys of the ocean's floor. Here marks the end of an era, to create a pace for a new, grander age.

Guidelines: In order for the new life to begin, the old must be swept away. You can swallow your pride, stand in your truth, and accept your new role, or not. Either way, change is upon you and cannot be stopped, or can the course be changed. Know that the light at the end of the tunnel is real. It will not be shut off due to budget cuts, nor is it the flash of a gun. Follow the light as it leads you to safety.

Reversed: You cannot stop the earth from spinning, nor can you stop the river's flow. Time waits for no one, so it's best you get with the program. The changes will not be disruptive, nor will they derail you if you just allow the current to take you to your next harbor. These are the changes you have been waiting for. They may not be what you expected, but they are exactly what you need.

Notes:

19 Hope

Have faith; there is always hope.

Here is the bridge between "Chaos" and "Inspiration." Number 19 brings all into focus.

Into every life comes the pain and suffering of loss. The loss can come in various forms, from the loss of one's house keys to the loss of a beloved family member or pet. We can lose our way, lose time, or lose any number of possessions, ideas, or things we hold dear and consider being of value. The evolution of great loss will then lead us to grief. When we experience deep, personal loss, it is natural to grieve. Grief can be all consuming and overwhelm even the staunchest of those among us. We also know during these times that it must run its course, since we have few options except to experience each stage of grieving. But through it all, the one thing that remains when we stop to look is "hope." This is the eternal promise to those who have lost and grieved from the very fiber of their beings to the depths of their souls. Imagine if you woke up tomorrow morning with no home, no possessions, no money, or even no one. All that would be left would be whether or not you would give in to despair and allow depression to swallow you, or would you begin to look for what remains and find hope?

This experience of loss is so ingrained in the human psyche that it has been memorialized in songs, stories, and, in more-recent times, videos. One term that comes to mind is "the dark night of the soul." This goes back a very long way in time and is often described as when all perceived meaning in life has collapsed. This leaves a lasting impact and forces one to reevaluate and reconsider what is and is not important in life. Or not . . . You can always curl up in a ball, pull a blanket (if you have one) over your head, and wallow in self-pity. But after a while, that gets boring and you start looking around for something to do. This is where certain things might attract your attention. This is where you take stock of what remains, and count your blessings. Even if there's only one blessing, that's one more than you thought you had not so long ago. So take that blessing and wipe the dirt, tears, and snot off it to shine it up a bit. There, that's better. Now, it needs a name. How about you call it what it is? Hope.

Shadows of gray bleed from the desolation of the forest into the sky above. Smoke and ash clog the once-pristine stream and poison the life beneath the waters. Bare branches, blackened and skeletal, appear to claw away from the destruction left by hell's own fires. Yet, in a small clearing near the heart of the once-bountiful woodland, the beating of wings softly stirs the air. Gently riding the currents, a single snow-white Dove weaves her way toward the carefully tended nest on the ash-covered ground. Safe in the nest, two small eggs glowing with iridescent light guide her home. Although surrounded by decay, death, and destruction, the mother Dove returns to nurture and protect what remains of tomorrow's promise.

Guidelines: Hope allows you to approach life's challenges with the confidence and surety that there is no problem without a solution. No matter what has happened, take the time to reevaluate your current situation. One by one, count your blessings and gather what remains of your resources. There is always enough to begin again. Have faith, since there is always hope.

Reversed: When all hope seems lost, allow yourself time to grieve before searching for a solution. Hope is not lost; it is only waiting quietly for you to recognize its presence. Reflect on the past and remember what it took to get you to the here and now, and take heart. Remember too that you have always found a way to move on. Even when the darkness threatened to consume you, you survived.

Notes:

20 Inspiration

Nurturing your muse will bring what is needed.

Inspired by the Tarot's "The Star," number 20 honors those born to be in service.

During times of creativity, we often feel our personal muse guiding our thoughts and actions. These periods of innovation are often accompanied by altered perceptions of time. When engaged in something inventive, our imagination knows neither bounds nor restrictions of time and space. This applies to all forms of art and all creative endeavors. From the solitary painter secluded in the well-lighted attic to the architects of the wondrous pyramids, we each feel the divine influence communicating sacred revelations. During these episodes of inspired innovation, we often forget to eat, sleep, or feed the cat. The Muse of Inspiration can often take over your existence, where days, weeks, or even months can pass in a blaze of insight, vision, and artistry. These episodes can leave you famished and often a bit punchy from sleep deprivation. However, the results will inevitably surpass your original vision when viewed from the other side of the creative mountain your muse has dragged you over . . . so long as you allow inspiration to guide you and not be solely motivated by the promise of a paycheck at the end of the trail.

There is a noticeable difference between truly inspired creations and those that are manufactured to pay the bills. Yes, paying the bills is important. There are few deterrents as demanding as not having the necessities of life provided. But it shows in your work if it's forced or the project is simply not within your personal field of inspirational subjects. If your heart and dreams beckon you to paint glorious landscapes, doing an architectural drawing may not be your forte. Forcing the process not only shows in the final piece, it actually glares at the viewer like the mythical basilisk. So, you might ask how do you overcome this necessity and still maintain your artistic integrity. You do so by courting your muse. Take your muse out and walk barefooted through the woodlands. Read books, or watch movies and share popcorn with your muse. Pet the cat. Pet the dog. Teach your goldfish to sing. No, scrap that. You'll only waste your time and annoy the fish. But any or all of the things that feed your soul also feed your muse. See? Everyone wins and everyone's happy. It can also be beneficial to introduce your muse to your closest friends. They, in turn, can share their muses with you, and (wait for it) everyone can be amused.

When you create from the heart, your works speak a language of the soul that can transcend words and speak directly to the hearts of others.

A spectacular sunrise paints the sky in colors only nature can assemble. Six diamond-brilliant stars hang in the heavens while a seventh rests delicately in the upturned palms of a maiden. In the distance, a solitary heron sends a message of intelligence, independence, and self-determination to those who listen. Three Star Flowers decorate the maiden's hair and symbolize the delicacy of love in this fleeting, fragile, present moment, while the palm leaves promise peace and eternity. The Muse of Inspiration crosses her legs and tucks her feet to mimic the petals of the lotus, symbolizing her unity with eloquence and divine energy. From her cupped hands flow the eternal waters of angelic inspiration to nurture those who create from inspired imagination. A pacific breeze playfully lifts her auburn mane while whispering insights and encouragement to pass on to the aspiring dreamers.

Guidelines: Glistening bubbles of inspiration burst free of the murky depths of the mundane and rise to the surface to bloom as the water lily strives for the sun. Inspiration is within you and can be nurtured with imagination if you free your thoughts from doubt. Pay particular attention to your inner voice, then listen closely to the song your heart sings.

Reversed: The feelings of hopelessness and helplessness are dual signs of the same fear. You have embraced victimhood, and it does not serve who you truly are. Although loss and despair are present, do not allow this to define you. You have within your soul what is needed for true peace and true vision. Now is the time to court your Muse and begin to creatively redefine yourself.

Notes:

21 Intuition

Where the Sun gives us life, the Moon gives us Dreams.

Inspired by the Tarot's "The Moon," the number 21 represents the fulfillment of a difficult process of spiritual transformation.

When the light of spirit shines brightly within us, it is reflected throughout our lives. It guides us, offers counsel, and is sometimes heard subliminally as the still, small voice from within. This direct link to the pure light of divinity and the All That Is is what we often refer to as "intuition." Although intuition is an innate ability, it is also like a muscle and needs to be exercised and strengthened to be of consistent, reliable service. To hone our intuitive skills, we must learn to distinguish the subtle difference between what are authentic intuitive "hits" and knee-jerk, fear-based reactions. An authentic intuitive message will have a feeling of "rightness" to it. This type of knowledge will give you calm assurance and a comforting feeling within the center of your body. The other one, the fear-based reaction, will make you feel pushed into doing something you're not sure about. These fill you with anxiety and are always founded on negative past experiences. It's up to each of us to learn the differences and work with what serves us and those we care about.

Intuitive guidance, also called "hunches," can easily be nurtured and developed into very reliable tools. Mundane history and past experiences block authentic spiritual enlightenment from entering our awareness, much like the earth can block the light from the sun to the moon. One of the simplest ways to tell which is which can be done by waiting. If you get the overwhelming feeling you need to call, see, or do something, and you're not positive it's your intuition checking in, just wait. Take a few deep breaths and calm your heartbeat and your mind. If the feeling returns, note where it's entering your body. Then again, let it go. If it returns three times, you have an authentic intuitive message that definitely needs your attention. This will help you develop your intuition and refine it. You will soon have a valuable, dependable sentinel that is always alert and ready to be of service as a well-trained guard dog. This is opposed to a neurotic pest, whose yapping at shadows is as useful as chasing its own tail.

Illuminated by the full moon, a young woman sits on the root of an eternal, sacred yew whose gifts include granting passage to the other realities. Here she receives messages from other worlds, as shown by the numerous stars that arise sparkling from the innermost reaches of antiquity. An enduring spring flows from the hollow into the pond whose waters bestow emotional depths to the messages from the other worlds. An otter floats on the surface, bringing adaptability in difficult situations and the assurance that you will be comfortable in the depths of this most divine feminine encounter. Dressed in a blue silken gown, the woman has achieved mastery over her fears and allows only truth to enter her being. Subtle tattoos of leaves decorate her face and trail down her shoulders, depicting her connection with Nature. A hibiscus adorns her hair, symbolizing the delicate beauty of what we have named "intuition."

Guidelines: A time of transition and change is upon you. Listen carefully and closely to the inner voice of your intuition to know which steps to take. A safe passage can be found only if you are willing to trust what you know to be true. Be fearless in your beliefs, but also ready to embrace new thought. Look deeper to see the truth of the situation.

Reversed: You and only you are responsible for your happiness. Release what causes sorrow, and embrace what brings joy. Unsolved mysteries are waiting to be brought into the light. It is up to you to dream the truth into being. Dive into the river of consciousness and float along the currents of authentic emotions. Let your subconscious guide you to a safe haven.

Notes:

22 Heart Song

Find what makes your heart sing.

Inspired by the Tarot's "The Sun" card, "number 22 turns lofty dreams into reality.

It has been my experience that children view the world as a place of wonder and discovery. They often dance, sing, and play with wild abandon, not caring who watches or approves. As they learn to communicate, their innocent wisdom can be both insightful and profound. Additionally, their views can be unique, to the point of stumping even the most-attentive parents and guardians. A trip to the zoo, the park, or even the grocery store can become a wonderland of new insights and perceptions when accompanying a toddler on their first visit. As adults, we've been to zoos multiple times, and what may seem to us to be simply a giraffe becomes a magical creature with a long, black tongue that delights the little ones into stories and speculation as to why this is so. A playground at the park may become pirate adventure while sailing the Seven Seas on a field of grass. The grocery store becomes a magic kingdom of colors and smells that have small hands reaching for cans of caviar with a delighted "What's this fish?," much to the shock of the parent.

All too soon they grow beyond their need for our constant care and attention. With each new day, they take the magic of discovery along with them as they journey to adulthood. But that doesn't have to be. As they and we grow and explore, we all can choose to keep that childlike wonder alive and flourishing. We can look anew at what we've seen a thousand times, and deeply appreciate that person, the place, or the situation that once brought such joy. We can conjure deep gratitude for the things that truly matter in our lives. We can hold close the openness to explore new ideas and not prejudge or allow our past to color our future. We can color outside the lines, turn an empty box into a fort, or jump into puddles rather than daintily mince around them. We can choose to be happy. We can decide to skip being adults and go straight from our first to our second childhoods. This doesn't disallow responsibilities. Instead, it colors responsibilities with bright reds, passionate blues, and brilliant yellows.

A bright, golden sun shines down upon the wide grassy meadow. The cerulean-blue sky is lightly dusted with lazy white clouds sparkling in the crisp, clean air over the distant azure mountains. A small child in a royal-blue frock and a jaunty blue cap dances with wild abandon to the music of the wind, the sun, and his heart. Clutching a bouquet of sunflowers, he kicks his booted feet high into the crisp spring air while waving a crimson scarf about like a flowing banner. A silvery-white horse joins in the dance and prances alongside the little one. Both a guardian spirit and a symbol of pure power, the joyful steed lends strength and grace to the music within the child's heart. The horse also brings the promise that one's soul is racing its way to unrestrained freedom and now has the ability to travel the world, and the entire universe, at will.

Guidelines: The entire universe has added its blessings to your journey and is assisting and accompanying you on your path. Goodness, joy, mercy, and success are yours for the taking if you reach out and grasp the possibilities. Find what makes your heart sing and allow that song to become the background music of your life.

Reversed: The clouds have covered the sun, and all joy has vanished. Sadness and sorrow are your companions during this time of trial. Even though it feels like you've been hit by a bus or falling space debris, it is simply a time of low vitality and not the end of the world. Take heart and nurture the child within. Become the parent you need right now, and make some chicken soup.

Notes:

23 Rebirth

Once you step onto the path, there is no turning back.

Inspired by the Tarot's "Judgment," number 23 blends of the desires for knowledge, creativity, and diplomacy.

The fires of creation burn brightly when we discover the time has come to re-create ourselves anew. Often at these crossroads, we seclude ourselves in cocoons of privacy and solitude. We retreat into our inner sanctums, our sanctuaries, our wombs, to renew and reaffirm our commitment to ourselves and to who we are in the process of becoming. We begin by breaking down old thoughts and habits. Beliefs and truths are examined, dissected and, often as not, discarded along with worn-out shoes and broken dreams. Digging deeper into the foundation of our lives, we uncover "that which no longer serves," and if it cannot be repurposed or recycled, it will be thrown onto the pyre and consumed in the fires of destruction. These are times when mercy is not useful. This is when excuses are better left in the halls of preschools, and naked truths are exposed in the glaring light of revelations. Here is the true apocalypse of our journey as we uncover the purpose of the knowledge we have gained.

This is a time of regeneration and renewal down to the cellular level. It begins when you realize the person that others see is not who you are in truth. Consider that the human body is an amazing mechanism. It can and will heal itself of any disease or affliction if given the proper commands and incentives. We live in a world where the collective mind has agreed upon certain rules of engagement. In these accords, we are born, live, grow old, and die. Not because that's our fate, but because it's what we as a collective consciousness have determined. We each have within us the ability to alter, change, or reprogram these and all presets. This isn't an essay denying the existence of death and disease; this is simply another way. For example, as children we may see and hear things outside the "normal" range of perception. As we grow up, we're convinced by a general consensus that these things "outside normal" do not exist. As time passes, our imaginary playmates, friends, and magical adventures are gradually replaced with what's commonly accepted as "real life." But during times of rebirth, the rules change and it's Game On. Upon awakening, we understand the necessity of reinventing ourselves with passion, creativity, and intent. Here we give birth to ourselves in Human Form, personifying the words "Human Being" or "Being Human."

Against an indigo velvet universe sprinkled with glittering stars, a new life is born from the flames of creation. The newly hatched dragon lifts its regal head and opens faceted ruby eyes to view the world into which it has emerged. His golden crests and horns reflect the surrounding flames from which all life comes. For these are the Eternal Fires of Creation, and it is here we begin. As with any birth, there is underlying, undeniable aggression. As the mother strains and pushes to expel the child within, the child stretches and strives to escape the comfort of its womb for a greater life beyond. A passive spirit will never find the strength to emerge from the closed hard shell that sheltered it during the time of gestation. This period has now ended and the scarlet dragon emerges from its fiery shell, pushing, tearing, and clawing its way into life.

Guidelines: You and you alone are responsible for your rebirth. It is up to you to choose which form you will awaken into. Your life has come to an absolute where you must make way for new dynamic beginnings. Cast off the shell of your former self and embrace the life you were born to live. Changes are imminent and evolving down to the cellular level.

Reversed: Decisions made in haste reflect your fears of change. Put aside your doubts and allow your being to explore possibilities that were until now unavailable. The time of solitude has ended. It is up to you to awaken in your new form and step forth boldly into your new life. Become your own parent, mentor, and counselor and offer guidance to the one you have become.

Notes:

24 Attainment

Carpe Diem!

Inspired by the Tarot's "The World," number 24 is for diplomacy and harmony within all relationships.

Upon reflecting what it took to bring you to here and now, you should find yourself filled with a profound sense of gratitude. Knowing if one millisecond of one heartbeat had been other than what it was, you would not be you. And know that you are perfection. Consider all the worlds, all the countless choices, the billions upon billions of lives in creation coming together two by two to culminate in this one perfect being . . . you. Besides, you have to be you. Yes, it is a dirty job, but someone has to do it, and no one else is qualified. So get with the program and say, "Thank you." You are being offered an incredible gift. The Universe has been paying attention, and it's your turn to grab the brass ring. Yes, it's hard to believe because of the countless times you have circled on this carousel we call "life." Each revolution you watched someone else reach out and grab what you thought should belong to you. But then was not the time. And by now the reasons should be clear. At this moment, the only thing holding you back from accepting this wonderful opportunity is you.

This is when the personal freedom you have long desired is at hand. It has come at a great personal cost, but you have empowered yourself and allowed your consciousness to expand and encompass a greater truth. Having released the judgments, self-doubt, and guilt that held you in place, you are now free to move in any direction. To quote "The world is your oyster" would be an understatement. You are a part of, not apart from, all life and all creation. You are created from stardust, since that is the building block of life on our planet. So ask yourself, Are you less than the stars? Are you not as worthy as the squirrels or the bears? Do you not deserve to partake of all life has to offer? Stop asking yourself "why" and instead stand tall and say, "Why not?" Actually, that's not really a question but more of a statement. Say it aloud. Know it as truth.

The farthest reaches of the Universe coalesce to create our galaxy, our solar system, our world, and all that walks upon the land, swims the seas, and flies through the air. From the brightest colors of creation, the reds, golds, greens, purples, and blues, we are gifted with emotions and feelings with which to experience the fullness of this life. She watches patiently to see if you will accept Her Gift. The blue-green planet held in her outstretched hands bears the stylized image of the Tree of Life, showing us how to reach deep within ourselves to put down roots, reach for the heavens with our branches, bear fruit, and grow strong. She gently cradles us and our world, which glows with the light of spirit lighting our way across the darkness of the void. Her offering is held in open hands, waiting for each of us to accept the unconditional love with which we are created.

Guidelines: Personal freedom always comes at great personal costs, but what price do you place on sovereignty? You have arrived at a place in your life where joy, liberty, and independence are yours for the taking. Honor who and what it took to bring you here. Be grateful for all that was sacrificed for the greater good. It is your turn.

Reversed: When the fear of failure holds you back, ask yourself why you fear success. To stay where you are now would bring stagnation and, with that, delays, pain, and suffering. So what if your plans didn't materialize? Rather than quit, take stock, gather your resources, wait for a better opportunity. This is not the end but simply a redirection of goals.

Notes:

25 The Weaver

The web is what binds us together as well as the container that holds us.

Inspired by the Steele Wizard Tarot's *"The Weaver," number 25 brings introspection.*

Often we turn to divination when we seek a glimpse into our Fate or Destiny. Although the terms "fate and destiny" seem to be at odds with what we know is our free will, there is a purpose for all in the Grand Design. To summarize, think of fate as your heritage, location, and family prosperity or poverty. These are your birthrights or your inheritance whether it seems that way or not. Free will comes in when we choose how to express those birth gifts. How we respond will be woven into our life thread from birth to death. Just as each thread in the Great Tapestry is woven into the Cosmic Story, thereby contributing to the fabric of the grand design. Our threads can be strengthened, be loosened, and at times become tangled with others whose life threads interweave with our own. The Weaver can show us where exactly we are on our path. When this happens, it is accompanied by a deep knowing you are at the right time and in the right place; all else is a distraction. Here, the Weaver personifies the Great Mother whose weaving, singing, and dancing bound the Universe together, thus creating the connections between All That Is. Her web is the glue that binds us together, as well as the container that cradles us.

Although we perceive the experience of division, we are not separate beings. We need to remember that we are each a part of the Great Mystery of Life that manifests as individual awareness. At birth, we retain a fragment of the memory that we are "One," but the material plane's density and lower vibrations cause us to forget this truth. Here on earth, we as individuals can experience and express the uniqueness that we embody, allowing the All That Is to experience Its Self in exquisite detail. As it happens, the physical is the only plane of existence where this experience is possible. All we feel and experience flows back to the eternal source, to be added to the great cosmic stew of knowing. All life shares the same energy that is anchored in the center of each of our beings and connects us to the Creator of All Life. When we finish our quest in our body, the Weaver's job is to cut the silver cord to the physical realm, thus allowing our return to the Source of Creation to perhaps again experience a new incarnation, depending on our personal mission. Never let anyone tell you that angels and guides are the most-powerful beings to walk with you on this path. Only the bravest souls, the toughest spirits, will step up to the challenge of being human. The others are the cheering sections on the sidelines, so don't let them con you. We, as people, are the spiritual warriors gathering knowledge and experience for the Creator.

From the darkness of the Void, the Weaver sings harmony to the music of the spheres and weaves her silvery web, binding and connecting all points of light in the Universe. With her masterfully spun web, she secures our connection to the Source of All Creation. Her body is created from stardust. Her gown is woven from the colors of the night. Gossamer moonbeams gather to form her flowing hair as she pierces the veil with her haunting gaze. When each being's earthly existence draws to a close, the Weaver gently cuts the slender thread that binds the soul to body, freeing the spirit to return home.

Guidelines: The Web is spun. It is both the glue that binds us together and the container that holds us. Magic may influence the quality of the threads, as do authentic emotions. Each of even the most subtle vibration is felt by the Whole. Be aware of the music of the spheres and listen to the sound of your thread as it vibrates in harmony with All That Is.

Reversed: Your life has become entangled with another's or with circumstances beyond your immediate influence. This is not your true path. Raw emotions and an inflexible ego are adding to the confusion. You have given control to someone or something outside yourself. Reclaim your personal power. Identify where the web is broken, and find your own path.

Notes:

26 The Universe

The lifting of the Veil.

Inspired by the Steele Wizard Tarot's *"The Universe," number 26 represents creating lasting results for humanity.*

Being a part of the Universe is the essence of our truth as human beings. It is up to each one of us to remember that tidbit and behave accordingly. Throughout our lifetimes we will be asked: "Who are you?" What do you do?" How we define ourselves will be reflected in the answers we provide. Most people will start with their name and basic job description. This enables us to seek and find anchor points on which to build a relationship. Think of it as having an invisible grid you carry around in front of you at all times. With each encounter, we hold up our grids to see where the light comes through. If there are multiple points of light, chances are we can build a relationship on the matching squares of light. If there is little to no light, generally nothing ever comes of the meeting. This plays a large part in self-expression, self-knowledge, and self-mastery. Eventually, we learn to identify as "Being Human" as opposed to "Human Being." This small shift in self-definition redefines our idea of self away from the human aspect and emphasizes the spiritual aspect, thereby allowing a more perfect blending.

    We, as divine beings having a human experience, have the innate ability to stand directly in the center between Divinity and the physical realms. The heavens and earth represent two extreme points of awareness and vibrational rates, a bit like opposite ends of an industrial magnet . . . only times a *gazillion*. We're talking about as opposite as it gets when it comes to magnetic forces. We, being human, are to mediate the potentials and dissolve the barriers between these worlds. At this place outside time and space, we know these extremes can never be balanced, but they can be blended. It's our job to initiate communication and creation between the various aspects of "Being" by blending these energies. When we do this with mastery and grace, the flow between the two through us is seamless. With little to no effort, we can access the heavenly realms of knowledge and insight, bridging the illusions of time and space to apply what we have gathered into our daily lives and freely bestow these blessing to ourselves and others. Here and now, we are a part of the All That Is and an intricate functioning part of the Universe.

A glowing planet, filled with life, twirls and dances through the solar system. On its journey through the galaxy, it follows its assigned path as other heavenly bodies waltz along on their own voyage. The Universal Tree of Life anchors its roots deep inside the planet of its birth. Fertile ground, golden plains, rolling hills, majestic mountains, sparkling rivers, and vast oceans provide the essential building blocks for the Tree's earthly form. Growing and stretching toward the heavens, the Tree sends its branches out into the Universe, gathering light and sustenance to surge through its body and into its roots to nourish the planet of its birth. As a tree grows old, it produces seeds that contain its very essence. In this way, the tree becomes an immortal symbol of growth and strength. Thus, as we embrace our role in the Universal Dance of Life, we are ensured that the seeds we plant today will bear forth the legacy we leave to our planet and all life.

Guidelines: Along with great power, we also learn the burdens of responsibility. You no longer have the luxury of innocence or stupidity. You have stepped up and stepped into your birthright. You are now tasked with the privilege of being a direct link to the All That Is. Realizing and accepting the truth of who you are now has brought you to the attention of infinite powers that govern the universe. Don't screw up.

Reversed: Clutching the doorframe and digging your heels into the ground will not prevent the inevitable. You are going to accept the role you were born into, so you may as well put a smile on your face and do it. Yes, it is scary. Yes, it will change you. But you are ready for this. Check your ego at the door and stop blaming outside forces for your circumstance.

Notes:

27 Truth

The path of awareness.

Inspired by the Steele Wizard Tarot's *"Truth," number 27 has deep roots in compassion and tolerance.*

Truth is ambiguous at best. What is true for one group or culture may be completely anathema to another. Depending on your heritage, tribal customs, traditions, and teachings, your absolute truth might seem like a complete fabrication to another. But the fact remains that we as citizens of this planet have some core, generally agreed-upon ideas we refer to as truths. Depending on your moral fiber and belief structure, you have a very distinct set of beliefs that you define as Truth. We begin learning right from wrong very early on in childhood, mostly for our own safety. For example, when you're first learning to walk, it's not safe to cross the street alone. You must hold the hand of an adult in order to cross without harm. This is a great truth for a toddler. However, as you grow and gain wisdom, you should be able to distinguish if and when it is safe to cross a street. The traffic is still racing past the intersection, and the danger still exists. But a teenager reaching for the hand of an adult to cross a road is, one hopes, unnecessary. So as we grow, learn, evolve, and gain wisdom, our truths grow and evolve along with us.

At this juncture, we could go into the deepest depths and explore "truths" about killing, sex, responsibilities, religions, and other beliefs that pertain to different societies. But what really matters to each individual is their personal, core truth. The truth of what you feel and believe to be the highest pinnacle of human achievement. In order to live that truth, we must know that truth. Although simple in its basic form, each truth is tailored to meet the individual's needs. This is done through experience. By living and exploring we are each able to develop our personal truths. Once we have achieved this, we truly and wholly believe. At this point, if the entire planet stood up and disagreed with you, it wouldn't matter. Your belief wouldn't be threatened, because you have proven your truth to you. By the same token, if the entire population on the globe stood and agreed with you on the truth, it wouldn't make your belief any stronger. This is Personal Truth. It defines who we are, and if we live that truth, we can exist in a measure of grace.

While alone with her thoughts, the woman gazes into an elaborate hand mirror. Engraved on the back is the rune "Mannaz," representing one's self, which indicates it is time to go within and search for one's truest essence. She takes a deep breath to gather her courage and slowly lifts the ornate mask from her eyes. For the first time, she sees herself as she truly is. Unadorned and steadfast with no pretense or adornments, she looks at her reflection with open eyes and an open mind. This may be difficult, since we know the easiest person to lie to is ourselves. Without truth, without beliefs, we are left with a colorless world of gray mists and shadows. Only by removing the masks we each wear will our absolute truth be seen.

Guidelines: By acknowledging "Self" in all of your aspects, you are able to recognize your personal Truth. This journey of discovery leads to a belief in you that is founded in self-knowledge. When you believe in your own truth and reveal it for the world to see, standing in your truth becomes effortless. Your strength and courage allow you to fully live without prejudice or judgment.

Reversed: When you live by other's rules, you accept their truth as your own. What served you well before has become stale and shallow. What you once held as truth needs refining. There is also a need for soul-searching, reflection, and honesty if you choose to be true to yourself. Self-delusion has caused a conflict in a core belief. Find the strength within you to live your own Truth.

Notes:

28 Shadows

Embrace the inner darkness.

Inspired by the Steele Wizard Tarot's *"Soul Twins," number 28 brings cooperation and diplomacy.*

How can we stand in the light and not cast a shadow? The challenge here is to realize that the darkness serves us well on our paths. Each of us has said, has thought, and has acted in ways that we sooner or later regret. At the time, our words and actions may have felt and seemed justified, but upon reflection we realize that that is not who we are. In order to divert attention from what we believe was a despicable action, we may hide the facts or place blame outside ourselves by making excuses. During this period we may adopt a control drama to elicit sympathy or support from others. There is the ever-popular victim card, where someone or something outside ourselves forced us to behave in an unacceptable manner. This encourages the gathered crowd to feel sympathy. Other perpetrators may employ interrogation methods and ask ever-more-redundant questions, seeking answers that support bad behavior or suggest innocence. We might defend our actions with aggression, trying to force others to our way of thinking, thus making it acceptable to be stupid or wrong. Still, others become aloof or mysterious and pretend it never happened. But we all watched the cat miss the back of the sofa and disappear behind it with a thump. Nonchalantly strolling out and then stopping to groom your fur isn't fooling anyone. We all make poor choices. We all make mistakes. What happens next is what is most important.

People do not learn valuable lessons by always getting things right. Be it social norms, religious doctrine, or traditionally accepted codes of conduct, on occasion every person screws up. We may strive for perfection, thus ensuring tribal acceptance, but since we are being human we will not always succeed. The first step in growth is to admit and own what happened or what was said. The next step is to begin to correct the mistake. Be it a sincere apology or reconsidering offending comments, it needs to be acknowledged. If nothing else, you can begin with "Oops, my bad" and proceed from there. This is vital because once you've owned it, you have the power to change it. Begin with small steps and continue until your course is corrected. When you have achieved redemption, you can reflect upon the events and shake your head in wonder while you think, "That wasn't me." And you're right. That wasn't you. But now you know Who You Are Not and can get on with the business of being Who You Are.

Endless shadows form dark and twisting shapes in the eternal nothingness. From the deepest dark, a shape emerges and takes form. Eerily, an ebony dragon with eyes the colors of fire manifests behind the lone human adrift in the smoky gloom. Sensing a presence, the person's first thoughts dredge up primal fear from the depths of remorse. Panic freezes all movement, and the human is held hostage by terror. Slowly, breath by breath, gathering courage, the mortal being turns to face the demon from within. At once, human eyes behold the fragile beauty of the dragon with its flame-bright eyes, raven-black scales, and luminous silver horns. Recognition comes slowly as the veil lifts to reveal one's soul reflected in the eyes of the darkness. Gathering the night-black shadows into loving arms, power is reclaimed and wholeness takes root.

Guidelines: When we deny any part of ourselves, we deny wholeness. Become your own hero, mentor, and protector. Embrace your inner darkness and reclaim your power. You would not eternally punish a child for a mistake they made in the past. Do you not realize you also deserve forgiveness? If we are to truly become Warriors of Light, we must be strong enough to embrace the shadows we cast.

Reversed: When ego interferes with growth, you deny a part of yourself. How can one side of the coin cast disparity on its other half? Avoiding confrontation may serve you well unless it involves confronting your shadows. True courage is recognizing and acknowledging the fear and moving forward in spite of that fear. Become your own hero. Embrace your shadows.

Notes:

29 The Guardian

Allow only truth seekers to enter.

This represents the ability to communicate between the realms. The number 29 is for trusted companionship.

Often in our search for truth and enlightenment, we are confronted with what we might think of as roadblocks or, if you would prefer, plot twists. This happens to any and all who seek to discover and divine what lies beyond the physical realm. It's like making the journey to the top of the mountain in a far-off country to visit an ancient monastery. You have spent months or years preparing for this journey, and finally you have followed your sacred path. After a long, arduous trek, you arrive and manage to gain entrance to the holiest place to seek an audience with the Guru of Gurus. You wait patiently to sit at the feet of the Master, so Ultimate Wisdom may flow from their lips to your ear. Finally, the wait is over and you are escorted into the Divine Presence. With the greatest respect, you approach the dais and humbly ask for guidance and enlightenment. The Holy of Holies gazes upon you with knowing eyes and from a place of great love and compassion whispers, "Kid, you're just not ready yet."

What lies beyond the gateway are mysteries and unexplored worlds. To journey beyond, we must be ready to face the one thing that can defeat us . . . ourselves. In all the galaxies in all the universes and the multiverses, the only thing powerful enough to defeat you is you. That's it. That's all. When you arrive at this place outside space and time and confront your greatest challenge, it will be your ultimate battle. Here the war rages and victories are won and lost. "Why?" you ask. Because the spiritual warrior's greatest adversary is always one's self. We approach the battlefield with arms and armor, knowing in our hearts that the stakes are our own souls. Will you accept the challenge and meet your truth with strength and honor? Or will you cave and snatch defeat from the jaws of victory, blaming outside forces for your demise? To quote an unknown great Sage, "Suck it up, Buttercup." This is not a path for the weak. Only those who have survived the fiery forge, run the gauntlet, and banished the monsters will accept the challenge they themselves have decreed. With strength, honor, and integrity as your weapons and your shield, you will be ready to face any and all contests to emerge victoriously.

A seasoned warrior acts as the guardian of the gateway to the worlds beyond your borders. This is the challenge you have set for yourself to prove to you your worth. He stands before a stone portal inscribed with runic symbols (see *References* section), foretelling the trials and achievements of your soul's quest should you choose to continue. With his right hand, he draws the Sword of Truth, which clarifies thought and intent and dispels obscurity and injustice. In his left hand is the Oak Staff of Transition, as symbolized by the skull of a deer that is adorned with feathers from a raven, a hawk, and an eagle. Robed in dark-gray colors, the Guardian does not hold a judgment, nor does he have the desired outcome to the challenge you approach. His position is one of neutrality as he stands between you and the worlds beyond. He is here at your request to mediate your readiness to pierce the veil and transition between this world and the next.

Guidelines: You have arrived at a place on your journey where all of your strength and integrity are needed to continue onward. How you meet the challenges before you will determine your worthiness to proceed with your quest for mastery. Will you do battle with strength and honor? Will you stand in your truth and allow your convictions to shield you?

Reversed: More experience is needed before you attempt the crossing. The way is treacherous and fraught with danger. In order to guide others through this passage, you must first master the gate and become the Guardian. There are unseen pitfalls and false trails that will leave you searching for answers yet unasked. To put it bluntly, you are not quite ready to step through the portal to go beyond.

Notes:

30 Wisdom
The soul's truest knowledge

Although wisdom defies description, it is recognized when encountered. Number 30 represents unlimited goddess energy.

To live and act with wisdom is to truly be the human embodiment of spirit. As Divine Beings who are parts of the gods and the goddesses, we house these sparks of Creation within our human bodies. This enables us to think and act, using all of our accumulated knowledge, experiences, and understanding. It incorporates common sense as well as insight. Additionally, wisdom is often linked to compassion, self-knowledge, being nonjudgmental, and behaving ethically as well as with benevolence. When we live and act with wisdom, we transcend the boundaries between the physical and the heavens and exist in a blended reality that encompasses All That Is. Emotions become the tools we use to express our deepest desires, truths, and needs. Words are used to express our ideas, our thoughts, and our visions. We listen without prejudgment and form opinions on what is presented with merit. We see clearly what is before us, and can differentiate between what matters and illusion. When we embrace wisdom, we become more than we have been before.

Wisdom, if we care to look, comes in many forms and flavors. There's the wisdom of Nature that cycles birth, life, death, and rebirth as effortlessly and seamlessly as breathing in and out. This is reflected in the wisdom of our planet, which is very much aware and alive. There's the wisdom of the universe that magically, or magnetically, sends planets, stars, and all heavenly bodies along their designated paths, bringing beginnings and endings together in an ever-changing dance of creation. There is the wisdom of our bodies that, if we listen, will guide us through life healthy and productive. Then there's the wisdom of our ancestors. The wise words of those who came before us may or may not be seen as wisdom as we view it today, but without their existence, without their traditions, without their experience, we would not be able to temper our wisdom of today. Only by carefully considering the wisdom of All That Is can we understand our places and our roles. It is also wisdom that dictates that we cannot all be the wise one that dispenses wisdom to the huddled masses. Some of us need to stand on the sidelines to pay homage and applaud as the sage's chariot flows past.

In the distance, crystalline snow-covered mountains stand majestically against a cloudless ice-blue sky. The Timberline is shadowed in the predawn mist while the earth continues its stately journey toward daylight. A woman steps forth, neither ancient nor newborn. The Lady stretches her arm above her head to greet the day as she removes her silken blue veil covering her ice-white hair. In her right hand, she holds the Staff of Wisdom, carved from an ancient hazel tree that was chosen as its branches grew to form a lemniscus. As she lifts her face toward the light, her Familiar glides toward her on silent, ivory-colored wings. The Snowy Owl carries the gift of sight beyond the illusion. This exquisite Owl embodies the purity of intent, the essence of true wisdom, and can see what others cannot. True wisdom cannot be deceived.

Guidelines: You have gathered knowledge, experience, and learning and are now ready to make good judgments. You have listened without prejudice and weighed the outcomes of all decisions carefully with a clear mind. It is now time to state your opinion clearly, concisely, and without hesitation. You have applied common sense, compassion, and understanding of your decision.

Reversed: You are much too invested in the outcome to make a fair decision. It's not about winning or losing; it's about fairness and honesty. Basing your judgment on feelings alone will not provide you with a satisfactory outcome. You must employ compassion for all concerned to make a wise decision. True self-knowledge equals nonattachment, and virtues such as ethics as well as benevolence.

Notes:

31 Emergence
Knowing and claiming your true worth

Challenges are met and overcome. Number 31, in essence, is a sense of worthiness.

When you began this part of your journey, you felt diminished and depleted, and your purpose was not clearly defined. Your thoughts were scattered, and a case of brain fog worthy of medical attention haunted you. It felt like you were trying desperately to put together the multiple thousands of puzzle pieces that came to you in a well-designed decorative box, only to find that the pieces were from completely different puzzles. These times are reminiscent of the childhood determination to run away from home. You packed your favorite toys and perhaps some clean underwear. You deliberately let the front door slam and marched to the end of the walkway, determined to make your own way in the world. From there, you most likely sat on the curb, where sooner rather than later you became bored and hungry. Shortly after, you headed back inside, thus ending your grand adventure. As an adult, those feelings have persisted to some degree. More than once you considered giving up or running away. But you didn't do that. You persevered, and now it is revealed that in a most curious way, your stubborn tenacity has served you well.

Consider this: if it were easy, everyone would take this path. If the way were not fraught with danger and detours, you would have a veritable crowd traveling along with you, and there would be handy directional signs and rest stops. You might even be able to access an escalator or two, and the occasional shortcut that didn't involve having to learn a foreign language. Plus a wise native sherpa would be along to pack your tent and pass out water and energy bars. But none of these figures into traveling the One True Path. Why not? Because you know that it wouldn't be worth the trip to take the easy route. In spite of the whining and complaining, taking the safe path wouldn't test you. That path is for the masses, not for you. You chose this challenge, and behold—you have succeeded.

The darken labyrinth beacons you to "Enter at your own risk." You will never be more ready than you are at this exact moment. You take the first step, and the door to the past closes on the person you were, and you prepare to embrace who you are becoming. The path twists and turns as the shadows reach for your embrace. You gather your courage and trust your instincts to guide you. You proceed with caution, knowing you are answering the call of a higher purpose. After what seems like an eternity, you emerge at a new beginning. Beneath the ornately carved archway whose keystone bears the rune "Sowilo," for wholeness, the vista opens before you. A cerulean-blue sky is reflected in the snow-capped mountain as the misty forest stretches from the sparkling waterfall to the foothills. Open your arms, your heart, your mind, and your spirit to embrace the wonder of emerging from the darkness.

Guidelines: In essence, emergence portrays a coming into being. The trials and challenges of recent days, months, or years have culminated in bringing you to a place of respite, clarity, and peace. You have been tested and have proven yourself worthy to the one person that matters . . . you.

Reversed: Refusing to accept the responsibility of being who you are in truth. When you accept the role others assign you, you are diminished and your value as a person is lessened. Being small does not serve to make others larger. Face the darkness and face your fears. The path awaits your footsteps.

Notes:

32 Infinity

Eternity, wholeness, and completion. ∞

The lemniscate symbolize infinity. Number 32 brings a personal sense of creative freedom.

We, as divine beings experiencing humanity, will find it is not entirely possible to fully know and understand infinity. We chose this existence of finite boundaries and limitations to better understand and express the illusion of individuality because this cannot be done as pure spirit, which is, by definition, infinite. Yet, during our human adventures there is still what might be termed "a ghost of an idea" that there is far more to our sagas than what we can see, hear, smell, taste, and touch. It sits quietly at the center, patiently waiting for you to give it a nod or a wink. For those who are destined to follow a certain path, sooner or later you will be drawn to your calling. Something will happen that grabs you by the ears and forces you to look closely with both eyes. Some of you may even experience a near-death experience (NDE) and even leave the body for a brief tour of the beyond. During these times of intensity, everything can seem to be condensed into the expanded moment you are experiencing. Time seems to slow, and your surroundings are crisp, clear, and in 3-D. Every detail is etched into your memories, and as the events unfold, you may become aware of the feeling that you are being watched. At this moment, Spirit has entered and you are forever changed, because as of now you remember.

For the past couple of thousand years plus, philosophy and mathematics have striven to explain the unexplainable to our limited brains. In some cases, they would have better luck trying to get an octopus to play the bagpipes. But regardless, some of us have tripped and gone down that rabbit hole at some time in our lives. For example, my teen years were spent largely on horseback while avoiding school. This gave me precious time alone and afforded loads of time to think. I remember clearly contemplating division and wondering how far anything could be divided repeatedly, even beyond what the human eye could see. The answer I came up with was "infinity." Of course, after arriving at that conclusion I decided to go the other way and wondered how many times something could be multiplied before it was too large for humans to contemplate. Again, I arrived at the same answer. This leads to the question "Just what is infinity?"

Beyond the known universe the cosmos dances and spins in perfect synchronicity. Using the ebb and flow of stars, planets, moons, and galaxies, the Creator of All That Is weaves the Tapestry of Life with no beginning and no end. The subtle elegance of Divine Creation captures the music of the spheres in the chorus of all life, thus giving Voice to the Infinite. Infinity may be difficult to explain or describe, perhaps because it is meant to be experienced. To reach beyond our senses into the Void, we must first incorporate our essence into our daily lives. Only by Spirit breathing its essence into our bodies do we live. Only by allowing Spirit a Voice can we find our way out of the darkness. Only by Spirit's grace can we exist.

Guidelines: The expanded moment of awareness where we accept, acknowledge, and embrace our place in the Universe. The infinite "now" brings our thoughts, actions, and voices into harmony with the Grand Design. There is only this moment. Where there was a restriction, there is now endlessness.

Reversed: Time is a creation of the mind whereby we experience the fullness of the material plane. It is a coming to be and passing away, not that which abides. Where before there was nothing, there is now fulfillment. It is in the doing that you find creation. Do not let past moments define you in your entirety. Expand and express your truth as it is now. It is in "being" that you find yourself.

Notes:

32 Infinity

33 I AM

I AM THAT, I AM.

Inspired by the Steele Wizard Tarot's *"I AM," the master number 33 tells us all is possible.*

When we use the word "God," it is often as a placeholder for spirituality and that which is essentially indefinable. With consciousness as the foundation of all being, we must recognize that our purpose here is to develop our gifts of intentionality to become effective creators. When we can look at anything, anyone, and everything around us and know "I am that," we are recognizing our oneness to the All That Is. A bit over five decades ago, a wise man told me the difference between a Saint and a sinner was recognition. I didn't get it. Months later, it hit me that the Saint recognizes the connection to the Oneness and the sinner denies the connection. So going through life being "judgmental" and thinking we are better or worse than the homeless, the criminal, the psychopath, the spiritual leader, or the savior just shows us where we are not embracing the Oneness. Given the right circumstances, anyone would be capable of acting out their worst nightmare, doing heinous crimes, or behaving monstrously. The truth is we don't know what happened to cause the behavior. Oneness asks you to be aware of what you see, recognize, and judge. The only way we are able to see those traits is by possessing them to some degree or another. If it is determined that we do not in any way, shape, or form own those undesirable qualities, then we must face the fact that we hold a judgment on them, which is also not desirable. Oneness asks you to embody the present and be an effective creator by embracing your destiny. Only by acknowledging All can we achieve enlightenment.

    My earliest memory of this path began the summer I turned sixteen; I was in my bedroom getting ready to launch another epic adventure on horseback across the Nevada desert. We had gone to church that morning, as we did every Sunday, and I was contemplating God. Much of what was told to me didn't resonate, so I had decided to do some thinking to see if I could get any of it to make sense. Mostly it had to do with God the Father. My relationship with my dad was awesome, so I had issues with a vengeful god who would punish his children for eternity if they didn't toe the line. I knew Dad could get really mad at me, but holding a grudge for an extended period of time made no sense. And I was being told God's love was greater than a parent's love. So yes, there were issues. That's when I decided to ask God who or what God really is, and then listen. That's exactly what I did. As I sat and listened, I picked up a pencil and began to sketch an old man's face, complete with long white hair and beard, rather like the epic biblical pictures depict God. Then across the top, I wrote the words "God is" and waited. It didn't take long for me to get bored and wander off in search of adventure. Two years later I realized the sentence was complete. God, Goddess, or the Creator simply is. This revelation accompanied the words "I AM," which began to reverberate through my entire being in a continuous chant. I started to doze off as the words flowed together and through me.

Suddenly a large, single eye fills my inner vision. Surrounded by the fires of creation that blaze in an endless universe, the unblinking Eye of the Creator gazes at its creation. Cosmic ethereal clouds drift slowly past the Eye against a field of innumerable stars. The watching Eye represents a state of enlightenment along with deeply personal spirituality, and valuable psychological significance to the observer. When your eyes are open and you stare into the Void, do not be surprised if the Void stares back.

Guidelines: You are a part of, not apart from, the Creator of All That Is. Here, we acknowledge each individual as an intricate part of the Whole of Creation who has manifested itself in outward expression. You have realized your truest potential and are in a partnership with your own inner divinity. You are standing in your personal truth and living that truth moment to moment.

Reversed: You have ceded your personal power to someone or something outside yourself. The conflicts in one or more of your core beliefs have created barriers and caused a separation between you and your inner divinity. You are denying an essential part of yourself when you deny the creative potential of your Spirit. When you deny yourself, you deny love.

Notes:

Fibonacci Spiral

We are in Nature as Nature is in us.
We are all connected.

The Fibonacci sequence (spiral) is also known as the Golden Ratio or the Golden Mean. Its omnipresence and astonishing ultra-practicality in nature demonstrate its importance as a primary characteristic of the Universe. The Fibonacci sequence starts like this: 0, 1, 1, 2, 3, 5, 8, 13, 21, 34, and 55, and so on eternally. Each number is the sum of the two numbers that precede it. This simple pattern appears to be a built-in numbering system to the cosmos. This series of numbers gets its name from Leonardo Fibonacci, an Italian mathematician from the Republic of Pisa born in the twelfth century, around 1170.

Once you look and see the Fibonacci spiral, you cannot unsee it. From the structures of leaves to lungs, paintings to photographs, and seashells to sunflowers, this spiral is predominant in art, nature, and the cosmos. It will seemingly stalk your vision and haunt your awareness. Recognizing the spirals that pervade us, our lives, and our worlds is much like getting a song stuck in your head, only this one isn't going to go away in a few days, weeks, or months. Oh no, it's here to stay. So make some popcorn and settle in for a compelling adventure as we explore the authenticity and inner workings of our most intimate, enchanting natures both within and without.

We truly are a part of this magnificent Universe.

Notes:

From the Oracle's Creator

Before the *Eternal Seeker Oracle* was born, numerous ancestors had to agree to conceive and produce children that would eventually lead to my mom giving birth to me, Pamela Steele. After that event, over six decades were accumulated, accompanied by numerous experiences from the absurd and mundane to the magical and illuminating. In essence, I got here the same way you got here. For our purposes, we will think of it as careful planning by the Creative Intelligence that governs the Universe.

Now that that's out of the way, I'll let you in on a little secret: I never intended to do another deck. Not Tarot and not an oracle. After creating the *Steele Wizard Tarot* (released on July 31, 2007), I made the mistake of saying "Never again." This inevitably leads to my (then) nine-year-old-granddaughter wanting a Tarot deck. While I was mentally inventorying (and discarding) the available "suitable-for-children decks," she ambushed me. Innocent, cornflower-blue eyes locked gazes with me, and the question "Will you make me one?" came out of her sweet face. The "Of course I will, Sweetheart!" response was a grandmother's reflex, and the "never again" *Wizard's Pets Tarot* (released in March 2015) came to be.

Fast forward to late summer 2014 as I'm finalizing the proofs for the *Wizard's Pets Tarot*'s printing, and two of my dear friends asked if I would create a banner for the very first-ever Northwest Tarot Symposium. "I'd love to!" came out of my mouth, because the instant they asked, an image had popped into my head. The working title became "The Hermit Dude." Once completed, everyone who viewed "The Hermit Dude" asked, "Is this the beginning of your next deck?"

"No."

About eighteen months later, I was left unattended with my schedule and my desk cleared, which are two almost-unheard-of phenomena, and a terrifying prospect for those who know me well, I began going through my files and happened upon an idea I'd had for a painting a few years earlier. With arthritis being the bane of my existence, I had opted for a drawing tablet and Photoshop to satisfy my need to create art. So once again, I fired up my trusty laptop, and within a matter of days "The Oracle" for the Eternal Seeker was finished. After "The Hermit Dude" and "The Oracle," I relented and agreed I was doing another deck.

However, believing I might not live long enough and knowing I certainly do not have the time to do an entire Tarot, I decided to start with the Majors and see what evolved. As the images came into being, they each had a purpose and a title. From the traditional Tarot, the Archetypes grew into a clear, concise protocol that, although inspired by the Tarot, wasn't anywhere near traditional. Each image appeared fully formed in my inner vision and was accompanied by sounds, movements, and a different title than the original. To elaborate, when you create a Tarot, you *live* each and every card you draw or paint invading your life for the entire time you're working on it. There are moments when the card of the moment reminds you of the uninvited relative that refuses to leave. They show up, take over your house, eat your food, argue with your spouse, annoy your children, and drive your vehicle. Only with their tenure up do they move on, leaving you feeling like you've been dragged through a knothole backward. Or possibly rolled in a wet blanket and beaten with a rubber hose. At each stage, in each moment, your very soul is turned inside out and left feeling like you've gotten third-degree burns on every inch of your being. And those are the "nice" cards.

But all in all, someone has to do it. The Voice in the Darkness screams your name and you answer. It's that simple. Christine Payne-Towler and I had an in-depth discussion years ago on how we agree that "the deck chooses the creator" and not the other way around. I am here to tell you I Am a True Believer.

So . . . Welcome and be at peace. I do hope you enjoy your Journey.

With Strength and Honor,

Pamela Steele

Acknowledgments

Thank you to the amazing friends who took the time to write the promotional endorsements for the book/box. I love each one of you.

- **Erik C. Dunne**—artist of *Tarot Illuminati* and *Tarot Apokalypsis*

- **Ethony**—head mistress, Tarot Readers Academy (http://ethony.com)

- **Mary K. Greer**—author of *21 Ways to Read a Tarot Card*, marykgreer.com

- **Christine Payne-Towler**—"Tarot of the Holy Light," noreahbrownfield.com

- **Gina G. Thies**—creator of *Tarot of the Moors*; author of *Tarot Coupling*

- ***Inspiration*** original image courtesy of Katalin E. Csikos, creator of *HazelMoon's Hawaiian Tarot*

- ***The Traveler,*** Ronni Ebel, a.k.a. "Rebel" (December 3, 1972–November 20, 2017)—friend, confidant, and my adopted daughter, whose courage, humor, wit, and strength inspired everyone whose life she touched. Three days before her passing, the image for *The Traveler* nudged my creative Muse, and within a matter of a brief few hours the drawing was finished. I could feel Ronni's presence as clearly as I was seeing the card take shape. Thank you, my friend, and remember to save me a place for when it's time.

Resources

Wicca Symbols

Female	Tree	Gateway
Male	Fire	Time
 Spin	Fruit	Life
Success	Rivers	Love
Cauldron	Synchronicity	Sun
 Mountains	Truth	Moon
Luck	Energy	Star
Storm	Protection	

Elder Futhark
The Three Aettir

1ˢᵗ Aett Freyr's	2ⁿᵈ Aett Hagal's	3ʳᵈ Aett Tyr's
ᚠ Fehu (F) Wealth	ᚺ Hagalaz (H) Chaos	↑ Telwaz (T) Warrior
ᚢ Urus (U, V) Strength	ᚾ Nauthiz (N) Need	ᛒ Berkana (B) Growth
ᚦ Thurizas (Th) Thorn	ᛁ Isa (I) Freeze	ᛖ Ehwaz (E) Movement
ᚨ Ansuz (A) Wisdom	ᛃ Jera (J) Harvest	ᛗ Mannaz (M) Self
ᚱ Raido (R) Journey	ᛇ Eihwaz (E, Y) Stability	ᛚ Laguz (L) Flow
ᚲ Kenaz (K) Opening	ᛈ Perth (P) Female Energy	ᛜ Inguz (Ing) Male Energy
ᚷ Gebo (G) Partnership	ᛉ Algiz (Z, X, Y) Defense	ᛟ Othila (O) Heritage
ᚹ Wunjo (W) Joy	ᛋ Sowulo (S) Sun	ᛞ Dagaz (D) Day

These are the incredible Photoshop artists who create epic brushes:

Although many if not all of the specialty brushes used in the creation of the *Eternal Seeker Oracle* are unrecognizable in their final applications, these were the brushes I started with for skies, backgrounds, trees, and other incredible effects. My eternal thanks go to each of these creative artists and all of the others who take the time to use their talents so that those of us who use Photoshop and drawing tablets can produce exceptional results. The brushes were found by searching "Photoshop CS3 brushes," and many were located on "Deviant Art."

11_mountain_ranges_brush_39385
24_cloud_brushes_by_Mila_Vasileva
Beyond_the_Mist_by_midnightstouch
Charfades_Ultimate_Grass_Brush_Set
Cloud_brush_set_4_by_s3vendays
Clover_and_grass_brushes_by_carocha
Firebrush_pack
Flame_brushes_743_fbe048457cfab0a1aa4cd2a03901f1f1
Grass_brush_set_by_Shoobaloo
Grassy_brushes_by_evionn
High_res_tree_brushes_by_julliversum
KeithSeymour_DragonScale_Brush
Kuschelirmel-stock_trees_CS5
Lightning_Brushes_DarkDesign
Mm_meadow_ps_brushes_by_magpiemagic
Pixelstains Reptile Skin Brushes
Simen91's Star and Light Effect Brushes
SS-Leaves
Star_Brushes_by_DomosthenesVoice
Tree_brushes_by_vanillaorchids
Wheat_brushes_by_coby17

My deepest gratitude.

References

Danu—https://en.wikipedia.org/wiki/Danu_(Irish_goddess)

https://angelnumbersmeaning.com/

https://thoughtcatalog.com/daniella-urdinlaiz/2018/10/alchemy-symbols/

Numerology—https://affinitynumerology.com/

Runes—Elder Futhark, "Using the Runes" by D. Jason Cooper

Wicca symbols—http://symboldictionary.net/?page_id=364

www.heathenhof.com/the-elder-futhark-runes-an-instructive-guide/

www.refinery29.com/en-us/what-is-numerology-number-meanings

www.therunesite.com/elder-futhark-rune-meanings/

Quotes

Oracle at Delphi, https://classicalwisdom.com/culture/traditions/oracleatdelphi/

Lao Tzu, www.goodreads.com/quotes/1339572-when-the-student-is-ready-the-teacher-will-appear-when

The Emerald Tablet, https://en.wikipedia.org/wiki/As_above,_so_below#:~:text=%22As%20above%2C%20so%20below%22,Pseudo%2DApollonius%20of%20Tyana)

Horace, www.britannica.com/topic/carpe-diem

The Order of the Star in the East, https://en.wikipedia.org/wiki/Order_of_the_Star_in_the_East#:~:text=The%20Order%20of%20the%20Star,India%2C%20from%201911%20to%201927.&text=The%20founding%20and%20activities%20of,media%20attention%20and%20public%20interest

Holy Bible, Old Testament, https://angelnumber.org/what-does-the-number-17-mean-in-the-bible/#:~:text=According%20to%20the%20Bible%2C%20number,used%20a%20symbol%20of%20perfection

https://en.wikipedia.org/wiki/I_Am_that_I_Am#:~:text=Its%20context%20is%20the%20encounter,has%20sent%20me%20to%20you

African or Native American proverb, www.quora.com/Where-does-the-phrase-It-takes-a-village-come-from

Flip Wilson, www.brainyquote.com/quotes/flip_wilson_368469

Pierre Dos Utt, www.goodreads.com/quotes/16086-there-ain-t-no-such-thing-as-a-free-lunch

Rhonda Byrne, www.goodreads.com/quotes/7954960-what-you-think-you-create-what-you-feel-you-attract